Teachin' Cheap

◆◆

Using Bags, Sacks, Paper, & Boxes in the Classroom

Written by Linda Holliman

Edited by Janet Bruno
Illustrated by Terri Sopp Rae
Project Director: Sue Lewis

CTP ©1997, Creative Teaching Press, Inc., Cypress, CA 90630

Table of Contents

Dear Teachers,

◆ *Teachin' Cheap* is brought to you by popular demand. It is an accumulation of ideas I have used with students and shared with teachers in seminars and workshops throughout the United States. Teachers from all over the country write me here in Littleton, Colorado, and ask, "Is there a book with all of these great ideas?" Now the answer is YES!

This book will show you how to use inexpensive materials for a multitude of student projects that can be used with any curriculum area, theme, or skill. In fact, variations of each project can be used over and over throughout the year. These easy-to-make projects require very little teacher preparation, and students find them motivating and fun.

Teachin' Cheap is organized according to the materials used—bags, sacks, boxes, and paper. The reproducible shapes on pages 98-111 coordinate with many of the suggested activities.

The bag, sack, and box projects are perfect for organizing and storing student work. They can also be used for center activities and attractive 3-D bulletin board displays. There are five different paper projects: Flip-Flaps, Slit Books, Poof Books, Tri-Folds, and Fold-Overs. These projects allow children choice and variety in how they "show what they know" about a particular skill or topic.

The over 200 specific activity suggestions are just a start. You and your students can take these ideas, adapt them to meet your needs, and create new ones using the same inexpensive materials. This book is not the complete resource; it is only the beginning!

Sincerely,

Linda Holliman

Linda Holliman

Paper Bag Projects

◆◆◆

Inexpensive and readily available, paper bags are a perfect tool to use in your classroom all year long. They can be used with any grade or in any curriculum area and are great for individual projects and center activities. The bags can also be used to display finished work by pinning them to a bulletin board or placing them on a shelf or window ledge.

Most of the suggested activities are made with lunch bags, but paper grocery bags can be used when you need larger containers. Encourage students to recycle bags of both sizes for these classroom projects. Basic supplies for the bag projects are listed on this page. Some projects call for additional materials. These are highlighted in the project description.

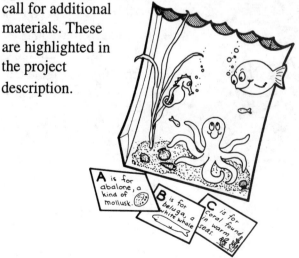

Lunch bags come in a variety of colors. Brown paper lunch bags are easy to find, and you can purchase white lunch bags in bulk at discount or warehouse stores. Colored bags are more expensive, but you can find them at party, craft, and school supply stores. Another option is to have students color or paint white bags.

When using decorated bags for center activities, laminate them for durability. Cut a small slit on the front of each bag, insert a paper clip, and attach labels appropriate for the activity. Write words, questions, facts, math problems, etc. on cards. (Or use the reproducible shapes on pages 98-107 of this book.) Have students sort the cards into the correct bags.

◆◆◆◆◆◆◆◆◆◆◆◆◆◆◆◆◆◆◆◆◆◆◆◆◆◆◆◆◆◆◆◆◆◆◆◆◆◆

Basic Supplies for Paper Bag Projects
• paper bags, various sizes and colors
• markers, crayons, colored pencils
• paint
• scissors
• construction paper
• glue
• tape

Anthill

How to Make

Round off the top of a lunch bag. Use markers to draw tunnels. Glue on paper or **plastic ants**, or use an **ink pad** and **ant stamp**.

Related Themes

• Ants
• Insects
• Animal Habitats

Related Reproducible

• Ant (page 99)

Activities

◆ After students hear *There's an Ant in Anthony* by Bernard Most and *Antics!* by Cathi Hepworth, they will be ready to start their own dictionary search for words that contain *ant*. Have them write their discoveries on cards and store them in their anthill bags. Older children can indicate the guide words found on the page.

◆ Read aloud *Amazing Anthony Ant* by Lorna and Graham Philpot to introduce or practice rhyming words. Have students write and illustrate rhyming words on cards and place the cards in their anthill bags. Encourage several students to get together to sort their cards by rhyming words.

◆ Number several anthill bags, and place them at a math center. Put plastic ants and a recording sheet in each bag. Have students make and record addition or subtraction problems using the ant manipulatives.

Apple
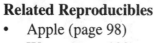

How to Make
Round off the top of a white lunch bag as shown. Use markers, crayons, or paints to color the bag. Cut a brown stem and green leaves from construction paper. Tape or glue them to the inside top of the bag. Add a brown construction paper worm if you wish.

Related Themes
- Apples
- Fall
- Nutrition
- Johnny Appleseed

Related Reproducibles
- Apple (page 98)
- Worm (page 102)

Activities
◆ Write short-*a* words on apple shapes (page 98). Place them in an apple bag and put the bag at a center. Have students empty the bag and sort the words into rhyming families (e.g., tan, man, pan; tap, clap, slap; pat, mat, sat).

◆ Brainstorm with students the many ways we eat apples (e.g., raw, cooked in pies and cakes, as juice). Have them draw their favorite way on a sticky note. Make a large graph on butcher paper, and have children stick on their responses in the appropriate rows. Ask them to write summaries of the graphing data. These summaries can be stored in their apple bags.

◆ *The Giving Tree* by Shel Silverstein is a perfect literature connection for an apple theme. Read aloud this classic to encourage children to think about ways they can share with others. Have them write their ideas on apple-shaped paper and store them in their bags. Take time to share their ideas.

Book

How to Make

Have students make a "book cover" on the front of a white lunch bag. Include title, author, and illustration. Add a cute bookworm with construction paper.

Related Themes

- Author Studies
- Library
- Favorite Books

Related Reproducible

- Worm (page 102)

Activities

- Give students the opportunity to share a favorite book with their classmates. Have students write a book summary or character description on the back of the bag. Younger students can draw pictures. Fill each bag with popcorn for snacking as students enjoy the oral book reports.

- Have students place small props or pictures relating to the book inside their book report bags. They can use the props along with a short book talk.

- Have students summarize a chapter of a favorite book on index cards. They can place the cards and the book in the book bag. Classmates can read the summaries to see if it is a book they might want to read.

Cactus

How to Make

Use a green lunch bag, or color a bag green. Round off the top and add "arms" by cutting and gluing on green construction paper. Use a marker to draw on cactus spines, or glue on **grains of rice** for added texture. Use **tissue paper** to make cactus blossoms.

Related Themes

- Desert
- Plants
- Southwest States
- Endangered Species
- Habitats

Activities

- Read aloud *Cactus Hotel* by Brenda Z. Guiberson to introduce animals that live in, on, and around cactus. Have students draw and cut out birds, mammals, and insects to glue on or store inside the bag.

- Create a desert display. Have students place research reports (e.g., desert plants and animals, desert ecology, desert land features) in cactus bags. Fill a large flat box or wading pool with sand, and "plant" the cactus bags in the sand. Invite students and classroom visitors to read students' reports.

- Have students work in small groups to make a desert alphabet on cards that can be stored in the cactus bag. Introduce this activity by reading *The Desert Alphabet Book* by Jerry Pallotta. Provide plenty of desert books for research.

Castle

How to Make

Cut turrets and towers on the top of a brown lunch bag to create a castle. Use markers and crayons to add special features such as a drawbridge.

Related Themes

- Castles
- Medieval Times
- Fairy Tales

Related Reproducible

- Rock (page 102)

Activities

◆ Read aloud *The Paper Bag Princess* by Robert Munsch. Have students make puppets to retell the story using the castle bag as a backdrop. Students can also write original castle stories.

◆ Have students work in groups to make replicas of "castle artifacts" (e.g., clothing, dishes, weapons). They can store the artifacts in large castles made from paper grocery bags. *Castle* by David Macaulay is an excellent reference.

◆ Use a large grocery bag to make a castle. Place books with castle settings in the bag. Add the castle book bag to the classroom library corner.

Cave

How to Make
Round off the top of a lunch bag as shown. Draw or cut and paste an opening and rocks. You have an instant cave!

Related Themes
- Geology
- Cave Animals
- Spelunkers

Related Reproducibles
- Rock (page 102)
- Bat (page 105)
- Bear (page 105)

Activities
◆ Bears hibernate in caves. Read aloud *We're Going on a Bear Hunt* by Michael Rosen. Have students write or draw the sequence of events on cards and place them in a cave bag for story retellings. Also encourage students to write bear hunt stories to share with the class.

◆ Study about bats, and have students use blank bat shapes on page 105 to record facts. The bats can be stored in the cave bags and used for writing reports or for class presentations. Students can embellish their caves by gluing bats on the front and at the top of the bag.

◆ Caves were man's first dwellings. Share pictures of cave art with students. Have them use the back of a cave bag to tell a story using pictures like early cave dwellers did. Children can exchange bags and try to read each others' stories.

Dirt

How to Make
Cut off the top of a brown lunch bag to create irregular hills or bumps. Add texture by gluing on **dried coffee grounds**. Add insects, worms, and other dirt dwellers drawn and cut from paper.

Related Themes
- Animals that Live In/Under the Dirt
- Plant Growth
- Archeology

Related Reproducibles
- Rock (page 102)
- Worm (page 102)
- Flower (page 101)

Activities
◆ Have students choose an animal that lives in the dirt to research. They can draw it, cut it out, and glue it to the outside of the bag. Research notes and reports can be stored in the bag.

◆ During a plant growth unit, use the bags as inexpensive planting containers. Have students line their bags with watertight plastic bags, place pebbles on the bottom, add soil, plant seeds, and watch the seeds grow.

◆ Go on an archeological dig together. Bury some "artifacts" in a sandbox or in the school yard. Let students take turns digging through the site. They can save any artifacts they find in their bags and make a presentation about their findings. Have children write about their "dig" and place the story in the bag.

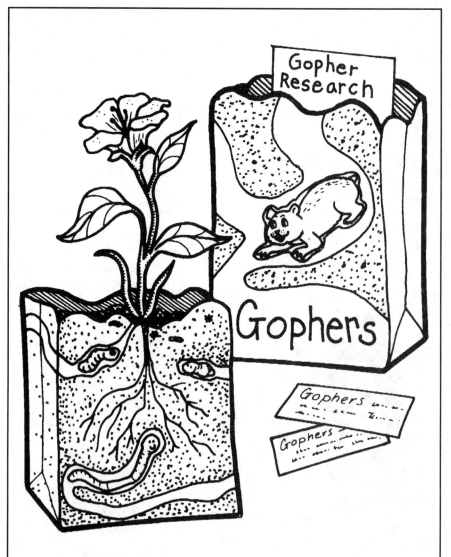

Doghouse

How to Make
Cut the top of a lunch bag to a point. Use markers or crayons to draw a dog in the doorway. Add the dog's name.

Related Themes
• Pets
• Responsibility
• Dogs That Help

Related Reproducibles
• Dog (page 103)
• Bone (page 103)

Activities
◆ Use the doghouse bags for a writing center activity. Make several doghouses with a different kind of dog pictured on each one. Brainstorm words that describe each dog. Write the words on slips of paper, and place them in the appropriate doghouses. Have students select a bag and write a descriptive paragraph about the dog.

◆ Have students write dog-care tips on bone or dog shapes (page 103) and store them in a doghouse bag. They can share tips and discuss responsible pet ownership.

◆ Have students write stories from a dog's point of view. Introduce this activity by reading *My New Boy* by Joan Phillips or *The Puppy Who Wanted a Boy* by Jane Thayer. Place the doghouses, with stories inside, in the reading center, or display them on a bulletin board for recreational reading.

Fairy Tales

How to Make

Cut and decorate a bag to resemble a house in a particular fairy tale.

Related Fairy Tales

- *Jack and the Beanstalk* (house with beanstalk)
- *Hansel and Gretel* (candy house)
- *Three Little Pigs* (straw, stick, brick houses)
- *Little Red Riding Hood* (Grandma's house)

Activities

◆ Have students make puppets for retelling a favorite fairy tale. Place the puppets and bags at a center.

◆ Collect several different renditions of four or five different fairy tales. Make a house for each fairy tale out of a paper grocery bag. Place the books in the bags. Pass out one bag each to small groups of students. Have them compare and contrast the different renditions.

◆ Have students draw the three little pigs' straw, stick, and brick houses on three different sides of the same lunch bag. They can rewrite the fairy tale from the wolf's point of view, write a newspaper article about the incident, or write a letter to one of the characters. Have them place their writing pieces in the fairy tale sack. Display the sacks for all to read.

Fence

How to Make

Draw a zigzag line along the top of a brown paper bag. Cut on the line, and use a brown marker or crayon to draw in the individual slats in the fence.

Related Themes

- Farm
- Ranch
- Garden
- Home

Related Reproducibles

- Chicken (page 107)
- Pig (page 104)
- Cow (page 104)

Activities

◆ Invite younger children to draw and store pictures of the animals in songs like "Old MacDonald" and "Down on the Farm." They can use them to dramatize the lyrics as they sing.

◆ Have students choose a farm animal and research what products it provides. For example, a goose provides eggs, down feathers, and meat. Ask the children to draw a picture or cut out a picture of the animal and paste it on the front of the bag. They can draw or cut out pictures of the products and place them in the bag.

◆ Use the bags to make a math center game. Write a number on each fence bag. Provide toy animals or use paper animals, and have students place the correct number of animals in each "pen."

Frog or Toad

How to Make
Use a green or brown lunch bag to make frogs and toads. Round off the top of the bag and glue on cutout paper eyes (or **plastic wiggly eyes**) and a tongue. Use a marker to add bumps on the toad, or glue on **Rice Krispies**.

Related Themes
- Amphibians
- Pond/Stream Life
- Garden Creatures

Related Reproducible
- Fly (page 100)

Activities
◆ Have students draw pictures of the different stages in a frog's or toad's development. They can use the pictures to sequence or write about the life cycle. Students can take home their bags and share the information with their families.

◆ Read aloud any of the *Frog and Toad* books by Arnold Lobel. Then have children write their own frog and toad adventures. Display the stories and frog/toad bags on a bulletin board with a pond background.

◆ Write facts about frogs and toads on fly shapes (page 100). Place a frog bag and a toad bag at a center. Have students compare and contrast frogs and toads by sorting the facts into the correct bags. Ask them to place facts that apply to both between the two bags.

Grass

How to Make

Use green lunch bags or color white bags green. Cut the bag off to the desired height, and fringe the top. You can also glue on paper insects or flowers or use **stickers**.

Related Themes

- Insects
- Plants
- Picnics

Related Reproducibles

- Flower and Sun (page 101)
- Ladybug and Fly (page 100)
- Ant and Bee (page 99)

Activities

◆ Read aloud *In the Tall, Tall Grass* by Denise Fleming. Using rhymed text, this book presents a child's view of creatures found in the grass such as ants, moles, and beetles. Have students draw these animals on the front of the grass bag. Ask them to write rhyming words from the story and store them in the bag.

◆ Make a set of grass bags to use in a math center. Write a number on the front of each bag. Or stick a number card on with Velcro. Write math facts on paper insects, (pages 99 and 100) and have students sort the insects into the appropriate bags.

◆ Use an insect theme to review punctuation skills. To practice using quotation marks, have students write a conversation between two insects, or a short story with dialogue. Have them draw the insects on the front of the bag. They can place their stories in grass bags for others to enjoy.

House

How to Make

Draw and cut a roof line on the top of the bag. Use markers or construction paper to add details such as doors, windows, and chimneys. Use **fabric scraps** for curtains or **tissue paper** for flowers. You can also make other buildings such as apartment houses, stores, or offices.

Related Themes
- Families
- Communities
- Shelter

Activities

◆ Have students make puppets to represent each family member. They can use the puppets to introduce their families to the class. Have them keep their puppets in their house bags.

◆ Read aloud *The Big Orange Splot* by Daniel M. Pinkwater. Have all class members make identical houses on one side of the bag. On the other side they can make "the house of their dreams," just like Mr. Plumbean did. Ask students to write about their dream houses and place their descriptions in the house bags. Display the bags in the classroom, and celebrate the differences in the houses and the children who created them.

◆ To practice mapping skills, have students make buildings found in your local community such as a library, post office, market, or gas station. Place the bag buildings on a large sheet of butcher paper. Add houses, streets, parks, and other local landmarks.

Mailbox

How to Make
Round off the top of a white lunch bag. Cut and glue on paper scraps for the door and legs. Personalize the mailbox with your name and decorations.

Related Themes
- Post Office
- Valentine's Day
- Letter Writing

Activities
◆ Use mailbox bags all year as message centers. Students can write each other notes and letters.

◆ Teach a unit on letter writing. Introduce the unit by reading aloud *Messages in the Mailbox* by Loreen Leedy. Have students practice different letter formats such as informal letters, thank-you letters, and business letters. They can keep the letters in the mailbox bag.

◆ Introduce our postal system by reading aloud *The Post Office Book: Mail and How It Moves* by Gail Gibbons. Have students trace a letter from the time it is mailed until it is delivered. Tell them to write the steps on separate cards and place them in the mailbox bag. Children can use the cards to show their families the sequence of steps for mail delivery.

Native American Dwelling

How to Make

Draw a ladder and a door opening on the front of a brown bag. Add texture to the "walls" with crayon.

Related Themes

- Native Americans
- Types of Shelters

Activities

◆ Pueblos were communal dwellings built by Native Americans of the Southwest. Have students make pueblo bags and then group them together to make a village. Information and research can be stored in the bags.

◆ Storytellers are an important part of the Native American culture. Have students create stories, using objects as props, to share with classmates. The props can be stored in the bag and brought out as the story unfolds.

◆ Corn was very important to the Pueblo Indians. Line the bags with plastic, add dirt, and have students plant Indian corn. They can use a few kernels or a whole cob. Plant the cob about two inches below the surface. Students can keep a log recording plant growth.

Penguin

How to Make

Round the top of a black bag, and glue on a white construction paper tummy. Add the eyes and beak with a marker or paper scraps. You may want to add some kind of food hanging out of the penguin's mouth.

Related Themes
- Penguins
- Antarctica
- Birds
- Sea Life

Related Reproducible
- Fish (page 107)

Activities

◆ There are many different kinds of penguins. Have students work in pairs to research and report on different kinds. For a related activity, students can write riddles about penguins on a flap on the front of the penguin bag. Classmates can lift the flap to check their answers.

◆ Brainstorm penguin verbs with your children (e.g., swim, slide, leap, hop, waddle, climb, splash). Write the verbs on fish cutouts (page 107), and place them in a penguin bag. Place the bag at a center, and have students write penguin stories using the words. Or have students work in small groups, acting out the action words and guessing the words.

◆ Read aloud *Tacky the Penguin* by Helen Lester, a delightful story with a friendship theme. Then have students list ways to be a good friend or ways to make a new friend. These can be stored in the penguin bags and shared with friends.

I stay close to the surface when I swim. My favorite food is krill.

Who am I ?

Adélie King Rockhopper

Pumpkin

How to Make

Use orange bags or paint bags orange. Round off the top of the bag as shown. Cut and glue on green construction paper leaves.

Related Themes

- Plant Growth
- Halloween
- Fall
- Thanksgiving

Related Reproducible

- Pumpkin (page 98)

Activities

◆ Group the pumpkin bags on a bulletin board to form a pumpkin patch. Add construction paper vines and leaves. Place student-made stories and poems inside. Encourage students to read each other's works.

◆ Involve students in pumpkin math activities such as weighing and measuring various-sized real pumpkins. They can also estimate and count the number of seeds. Have students write about these activities in math journals and keep them in their pumpkin bags along with any special materials.

◆ Have students write or draw on cards or pumpkin cutouts (page 98), the sequence of steps from planting a pumpkin seed to creating a jack-o'-lantern. They can take the cards home in their pumpkin bags and sequence the steps for their parents. Let older students observe the decomposition of a jack-o'-lantern and record the changes in a science log.

Thunderstorm

How to Make

Draw or cut and paste clouds, lightning, and raindrops on the front of a brown or white lunch bag. Or make clouds by gently pulling apart **cotton balls**. Dust them lightly with **black powdered paint**.

Related Themes
- Weather
- Feelings

Activities

◆ During the rainy season, have students collect newspaper weather reports for a week or two, and store them in their thunderstorm bag. Ask them to record the daily temperature at school on the back of the thunderstorm bag.

◆ Have students write fantasy stories or myths about what causes thunder and place them in thunderstorm bags. Display the bags and stories on a bulletin board with rain clouds in the background.

◆ Read aloud *Thunder Cake* by Patricia Polacco. It's a wonderful story about a little girl whose grandmother has an ingenious way to help allay her fear of thunder. Have each student make a thunderstorm bag. Divide the class into ten groups. Have one student control the light switch (the lightning). As you read the story again, have students count along each time the lightning strikes. Ask each group to blow up their thunder bags, hold them tight, and pop them at the appropriate time. It's noisy but fun!

Water

How to Make
Draw waves on the front of blue or white bags, and cut the top of the bag as shown. Glue **sand** and tiny **seashells** to the bottom of the bag. Add fish cutouts or **stickers**.

Related Themes
- Ocean
- Water Cycle
- Lake, Pond
- River

Related Reproducible
- Fish (page 107)

Activities
- Share the following Jerry Pallotta books with your class: *The Ocean Alphabet Book, The Underwater Alphabet Book,* and *The Freshwater Alphabet Book.* Have students work in pairs or small groups to create their own water alphabet books. Give each group 26 index cards. Ask them to write and illustrate one water fact for each letter of the alphabet. They can keep the cards in the water bag.

- Use grocery bags to make four large water bags. Prepare four different water experiments. Store the procedures and materials in the bags, and place them in the science center or around the room for a science "round robin." Have students take turns doing all four experiments. Students can record the experiments and store their recordings in their water bags.

- Ask each child to glue a drawing of a sea creature on a water bag. Have students write cinquains (five-line poems) about their animals or collect ocean poetry to place in the water bag.

A is for abalone, a kind of mollusk.

B is for beluga, a white whale.

C is for coral found in warm seas.

Sack Projects

Sacks differ from bags; sacks do not have a flat bottom. They are similar to large envelopes. Just like paper bags, sacks can be used for a wealth of activities. Add them to learning centers, or use them to jazz up skill lessons. Have students store information and activities inside the sacks. They can take home sack projects to share with family members.

Sacks come in different sizes and colors. The most common colors are white and brown, but you can also find colored sacks in variety packages at some school supply stores. Check the yellow pages under *Paper* for companies that manufacture sacks. Ask for card or merchandise sacks. You usually have to purchase them in bundles of 500, but don't let that scare you! A class of 25 students can quickly use 500 sacks. Or, share them with a colleague. Here is a good source:

Xpedx paper store
1-800-351-8117

Basic supplies for sack projects are listed on this page. Some projects call for additional materials. These are highlighted in the project description.

Several projects recommend binding the sacks together to make books. There are several ways you can do this.

- Use staples if you are only binding a few sacks.
- Use a spiral-binding machine.
- Hole-punch the sacks and tie them together with ribbon, yarn, or string.
- Hole-punch the sacks and use paper fasteners. Put tape over the prongs on the back to keep them in place.

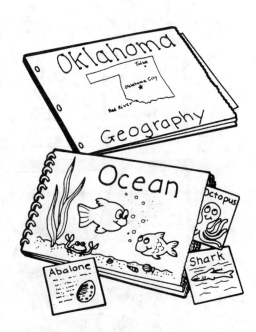

Basic Supplies for Sacks
- sacks, various sizes and colors
- markers, crayons, colored pencils
- paint
- scissors
- construction paper
- glue
- tape

Barn

How to Make
Cut off the corners at the top of a red sack to make the roof of the barn. Use construction paper to make a silo. Glue it on to the back of the sack. On the front, draw or glue paper barn doors.

Related Themes
- Farm
- Food Production
- Old MacDonald

Related Reproducibles
- Pig (page 104)
- Cow (page 104)
- Chicken (page 107)

Activities
◆ Make several barn sacks. Put a picture of a farm animal on each sack (e.g., hen, cow, pig). Have children draw or cut out pictures of foods that come from animals, such as milk, ice cream, butter, bacon, and ham. Place the barn sacks and the pictures at a center. Have students sort the pictures into the correct sacks.

◆ Have students use the barn sack to store a copy of the lyrics for "Old MacDonald." They can draw pictures (or make puppets) of all the animals along with Old MacDonald and sequence these pictures while singing the song. For beginning reading, give students small sentence strips and word cards to match to the lyrics.

◆ After reading *Charlotte's Web* by E.B. White, have students draw and cut out the main characters in the story. Ask them to write character descriptions on index cards and place them in the sack.

Bear

How to Make

Round off the top of a brown sack. Cut out and glue on ears. You may want to use **felt** for the ears to add texture. Add the eyes, nose, and mouth as shown.

Related Themes

- Mammals
- Hibernation
- Fairy Tales

Related Reproducible

- Bear (page 105)

Activities

◆ Make small-, medium-, and large-size bear sacks to represent the main characters in *Goldilocks and the Three Bears*. Have older students rewrite the story from one bear's point of view. Place the stories in the appropriate sacks for others to read.

◆ Read aloud *Ira Sleeps Over* by Bernard Waber. Have the children write about a sleep-over experience and make a sack to resemble a favorite teddy bear.

◆ Have students decorate a sack to look like their favorite kind of bear (e.g., grizzly, panda, or polar bear). Ask them to write five to ten facts about this bear on blank bear shapes (page 105). The facts can be stored in the bear sack.

Bird Nest

How to Make

Use a brown sack. Cut a nest shape and glue any loose edges. Glue on **grass, sticks, yarn,** and other **nesting materials.**

Related Themes

- Birds
- Animal Homes
- Life Cycles

Activities

- ◆ Make and laminate ten nests (numbered 1-10) for a math center activity. Make baby birds using tongue depressors, construction paper, and pipe cleaners for beaks. Students can use the birds and nests to sort by fact families as they place the birds in the correct sacks.

- ◆ Grow a bird nest in your classroom. Place a real, abandoned nest in a shallow bowl. Pour water in the bottom of the bowl, and place the nest in a sunny window. The nest will absorb the water, and the seeds in the nest will sprout. Have students make predictions and record observations in journals which can be kept in the sack nests.

- ◆ In early spring have students make and take home sack nests. Ask them to collect items that might be useful for birds building real nests (e.g., yarn, string, cotton, fabric). When the materials are returned to school, place them in mesh bags and hang them on bushes and trees around the playground.

Dog

How to Make
Round off the top of a white, brown, yellow, or red sack. Decide what kind of dog you want to make. Cut ears and a tongue out of construction paper. Draw eyes and a nose. Add spots or other markings.

Related Themes
- Pets
- Dog Stories

Related Reproducibles
- Dog (page 103)
- Bone (page 103)

Activities
◆ On the hundredth day of school, have each student make a dog sack with 100 spots using a marker, paint, or self-stick dots. They can place a collection of 100 small items in their sacks. Have them exchange sacks and recount the objects by twos, threes, fives, or tens.

◆ Read aloud *Clifford the Big Red Dog* by Norman Bridwell. Find the largest sack you can; paint it red; add eyes, ears, a nose, and a mouth; and hang it in the middle of a bulletin board. Tie yarn through the center of other Clifford paperbacks, and hang them on the board. Have students make small Clifford sacks and write original stories about Clifford. Place the stories in the sacks, and add them to the display.

◆ Read aloud *I'll Teach My Dog 100 Words* by Michael Frith. Invite students to collect all the dog-related words they know. Have them write words on blank bone shapes (page 103) and store them in their dog sacks. Students can place the word cards in alphabetical order or use them for creative writing and spelling practice.

Elephant

How to Make
Color or sponge-paint a white sack gray, and glue large construction paper ears to the back of the sack. Draw or glue on **wiggly eyes**, and add an accordion-fold paper trunk.

Related Themes
- Circus
- Zoo
- Endangered Animals
- Animals That Work

Related Reproducible
- Peanut (page 106)

Activities
◆ Have children research Asian and African elephants and make a sack elephant to represent each one. (One will have larger ears.) Ask students to write facts about both kinds and place them in the appropriate sacks. Students can use the information to make a Venn diagram.

◆ Have students use the elephant sack to collect long- and short-vowel *e* words. They can write the words on the peanut shapes on page 106. Encourage them to work with a partner to sort the words by vowel sound (e.g., short *e*, long *e*).

◆ Read aloud *Elmer* by David McKee, the story of an elephant who was a patchwork of brilliant colors. Students can create their own fanciful sack elephants and write stories about them on colorful paper. Place the stories in the sacks and display for all to read.

Flyswatter

How to Make

Use a marker to draw a wide border around the edge of a white sack. Use a fine-tip pen or pencil to draw the "screen." Add a paper handle at the opening of the sack. Glue a paper or **plastic insect** on the flyswatter.

Related Themes

- Flies
- Insects

Related Reproducibles

- Fly (page 100)
- Bee (page 99)

Activities

◆ Read aloud *Old Black Fly* by Jim Aylesworth, an alliterative alphabet book. Have students make flyswatter sacks. Ask them to write alliterative sentences that match the pattern in the book and place them in their bags. (E.g., *Old Black Fly balanced on a balloon. Shoo fly, shoo fly, shoo!*) Display the bags, and invite students to use classmates' sentences to create their own *Old Black Fly* books.

◆ Read aloud *The Icky Bug Book* by Jerry Pallotta. Have students work in groups to write and draw about insects from A to Z on index cards. They can store the cards in a flyswatter sack and quiz each other on insect facts.

◆ Create a bulletin board titled *Insect Pests, Insect Helpers*. Students can research insects in each category and illustrate them on their sacks. Place the reports in the sacks, and display them on the board.

Mouse House

How to Make
Make a mouse house by rounding off the top of the sack and drawing or gluing a cutout paper mouse hole at the bottom of the sack.

Related Themes
- Rhyming Words
- Animals

Related Reproducible
- Mouse (page 106)

Activities
◆ Reproduce the mouse patterns on page 106. Have students write/draw rhyming words/pictures on the patterns and store them in their mouse house sacks. They can use the word-mice for matching and sorting activities, playing Concentration, or writing rhyming poetry.

◆ Read aloud *Seven Blind Mice* by Ed Young, an adaptation of the fable about a blind man and an elephant. Invite students to place small objects in mouse house sacks and then have friends reach in, feel, and identify the objects.

◆ Read aloud *Mouse Paint* by Ellen Stoll Walsh, a story of how three white mice use red, blue, and yellow paint to mix new colors. Have students explore color mixing too by kneading together small pieces of yellow, blue, and red modeling clay. Reproduce the mouse patterns on page 106. Have students color the patterns to show what happened when they mixed red and blue, and so on. Students can take home the colored mice in their mouse house sacks.

Pocket

How to Make
Use a marker, pen, or crayon to make "stitches" around the sides and bottom of the sack to create the look of a pocket. To make a fancier pocket, add **real fabric** or **wallpaper** cut to fit the front surface of the sack and attach a **button**.

Related Themes
- Poetry
- Riddles
- Marsupials

Activities

◆ April is National Poetry Month. Read and display the poem "Keep a Poem in Your Pocket" by Beatrice Schenk de Regniers from her book *Something Special*. Have students make poetry pockets, copy their favorite poems, and place them in their pockets.

◆ Use the pockets for riddle writing. Have each child place an object in a sack and write a corresponding riddle on the front. Plan a sharing time so students can guess classmates' riddles.

◆ To introduce a unit on Australia, place a large paper kangaroo on the bulletin board. Use a sack for a pocket. Each day, put a new fact or object relating to Australia in the pocket. (E.g., include a map of the continent, a book about marsupials, a picture of a joey, etc.)

What can make cars, houses, and toys and still fit in your pocket?

Purse/Wallet

How to Make
To make a purse, decorate a white sack. Punch holes in the top corners, and add **yarn** for a handle. To make a wallet, cut off the top two-thirds of the sack. Fold the sack in half.

Related Themes
- Money
- Shopping

Activities
◆ Read aloud *Lilly's Purple Plastic Purse* by Kevin Henkes. Lilly loves her teacher, Mr. Slinger, until he takes away her purple plastic purse. Have students make their own purses or wallets. Ask them to draw or write about what they would keep in their purse or wallet. Like Lilly, they can write notes to the teacher and put them in their purse or wallet.

◆ Make several purses and wallets. Put a money value on each one and laminate. Have students practice counting out with real coins the correct amount for each purse.

◆ Have students go "shopping" in toy catalogs. Tell them they have $100 to spend. Ask them to record what they buy and add up the total amount on the back of the sack. They can also figure out how much change they would receive.

Solar System

How to Make

Bind ten sacks together to create a solar system scrapbook, one sack for the sun and the moon, and one for each planet. As you "visit" each planet, have the children use different art media to create the planet on the front of each sack.

Related Themes

- Space Travel
- Science Fiction
- Outer Space
- Astronomy

Activities

◆ Read *Postcards from Pluto* by Loreen Leedy to introduce the solar system. Have students write a postcard addressed to someone back on earth telling what they have learned about another planet. Add the cards to the solar system scrapbook. Place the book in the classroom library.

◆ Use the solar system sacks to organize and store information about the planets. Ask students to write facts about each planet on index cards. Use the fact cards to play a game similar to Trivial Pursuit.

◆ Have students draw or paint the solar system on the front of one large sack instead of using ten sacks. This sack can be used to collect vocabulary cards with new words and definitions. Students can use the word cards for dictionary work, spelling, creative writing, etc.

Sunshine

How to Make

Color a white sack yellow and round off the corners. Or glue on small **yellow and orange tissue paper squares**. (Use watered-down glue and a brush.) Cut sun rays out of yellow, red, and orange paper, and glue them to the back of the sack.

Related Themes

- Summer
- Plants
- Weather
- Energy

Related Reproducibles

- Sun (page 101)
- Flower (page 101)

Activities

◆ Purchase solar paper at a nature, school supply, or hobby store. Ask students to collect small objects in their sunshine sacks. Have each child arrange the objects on a piece of solar paper and place it in the sun. When exposed to the sun, the paper undergoes a chemical change, so an image of the objects will appear. Children can make predictions, write observations, and evaluate the process.

◆ *Sunshine* is a compound word. Have students collect other compound words in their sacks.

◆ Use the sunshine sacks to prepare for summer vacation. Have students brainstorm a list of fun, educational summer activities. Ask them to record their ideas on cards to keep in the sack. Parents will appreciate this idea bank when their children "have nothing to do" in the summer months.

Television

How to Make

To make a TV sack, glue a piece of white paper on the front of a brown sack. Draw or glue on construction paper *On* and *Off* knobs.

Related Themes

- Communication
- Entertainment

Activities

◆ Read aloud *Mouse TV* by Matt Novak, the story of the Mouse family and how each member of the family wants to watch something different on television. They find a solution one night when the television goes out and they discover many other things they can do together. Have each child make a sack television, write or draw pictures of activities they can do instead of watching TV, and place them in a television sack. Students can take these ideas home to share with their parents.

◆ Older children can use a TV guide and write a weekly schedule of programs to watch. Or they can keep a log of programs watched for one week and store it in a television sack. Use the collected data to make a class graph.

◆ Have students summarize a favorite program as a writing assignment, or ask students to evaluate commercials that target children.

Creative Writing

How to Make

Have the students use the front of the sack for one of the writing activities described on this page.

Related Uses
- Rough Drafts
- Writing Center Activities
- Sack Storybooks

Activities

◆ Create a center activity for young writers. Glue a picture on the front of a large sack. Use a marker to label objects in the picture. Include descriptive words (e.g., fat, fuzzy, black). Have children write a story about the picture using the instant word bank on the front of the sack. Put the children's stories in the sack for others to read.

◆ Older children can use the front of a sack to make a story map or story board for an original story. The story goes in the sack.

◆ Encourage students to make a chapter book using sacks. Each sack represents a different chapter in an ongoing story. Write the first chapter, place it in a sack, and illustrate the front. Ask students to add new chapters. Bind all the sacks together to make a book.

Envelope

How to Make
Use sacks as "envelopes" for letter writing. Students can address the sack envelopes and design their own stamps cut from construction paper.

Related Themes
- Post Office
- Letter Writing

Activities
◆ Have students practice letter writing skills by writing letters to favorite nursery rhyme, fairy tale, or book characters. They can ask the character questions or give advice. Ask each student to address and stamp a sack envelope. Have students place their letters in the envelopes and bind them into a book. You can introduce this activity by reading aloud *The Jolly Postman* by Janet and Allan Ahlberg.

◆ Incorporate letter writing with science or social studies themes. As a thematic unit draws to a close, have students write letters to their teacher or families explaining five things they learned about the thematic topic.

◆ As students practice writing different types of letters (e.g., thank-you note, friendly letter, business letter), have them create a letter writing portfolio by keeping a sample of each in a sack envelope.

Math Sacks

How to Make
Sacks are perfect for storing manipulatives to help solve math story problems. Students can write the problem on the sack or place it inside. The reproducible shapes on pages 98-107 work well for this activity.

Related Skills
- Sequencing
- Problem Solving
- Addition, Subtraction, Multiplication, Division

Related Reproducibles
- various patterns (pages 98-107)

Activities
- *Splash!* by Ann Jonas is the perfect book for introducing story problem writing. It's the story of a how a turtle, frogs, a dog, and a cat jump in and out of a little girl's backyard pond. Have students draw a pond on a sack and use manipulatives to act out the addition and subtraction problems as you read the book. They can then write their own story problems on index cards and place the cards along with the manipulatives in their sacks.

- Place rubber stamps, sacks, and markers at a math center. Have students write a story problem on a card, place it in a sack, and illustrate the problem on the front of the sack. Students can trade bags and use manipulatives to solve classmates' problems.

- Read aloud *What Comes in Twos, Threes, and Fours?* by Suzanne Aker. Make a class sack book by writing a question on each sack: *What comes in 1s? What comes in 2s?* and so on. Bind the pages together. Invite children to find magazine pictures or draw pictures of objects to place inside each sack page.

Student Portfolio

How to Make
Attach ten 10" x 15" sacks together for each student to use as an organizational tool for collecting work samples. Store the sack portfolios in a large tub or box to use throughout the year.

Related Uses
- Monthly Themes
- Monthly Evaluation
- Ongoing Assessment
- Organizational Skills

Portfolio Ideas
◆ At the beginning of each month, have children label and illustrate the front of a sack. As the month progresses, make collaborative decisions on which work samples should be saved in the portfolio sack. At the end of the month, students can look over their samples and self-assess their work on a form or on the back of the sack. You may consider letting students take home their monthly portfolios and asking parents to respond.

◆ Have students make self-portraits at the beginning and end of the year to include in their portfolios.

◆ Take photos of classroom activities throughout the school year. Students can include the photos in their portfolios.

Reports

How to Make

Bind and decorate sacks to make portfolios for the current unit of study. Use large or small sacks depending on the activity.

Related Themes

- Science Themes
- Social Science Themes

Ideas

◆ **Biographies** – Have students organize an in-depth study of a famous person, using several sacks stapled together. Sacks can be labeled according to topics covered in the report (e.g., childhood, education, professional life, major contributions). Students can keep gathered information in the sacks.

◆ **State Reports** – Have students organize a state report using several sacks bound together. Topics might be geography, history, agriculture, industry, tourist attractions, and so on.

◆ **Habitats** – Give each student three sacks bound together. Each sack represents a different habitat (e.g., desert, ocean, jungle). Have students add information, drawings, and poetry to the sacks as they investigate the various habitats. They can decorate the front of the sacks with appropriate illustrations.

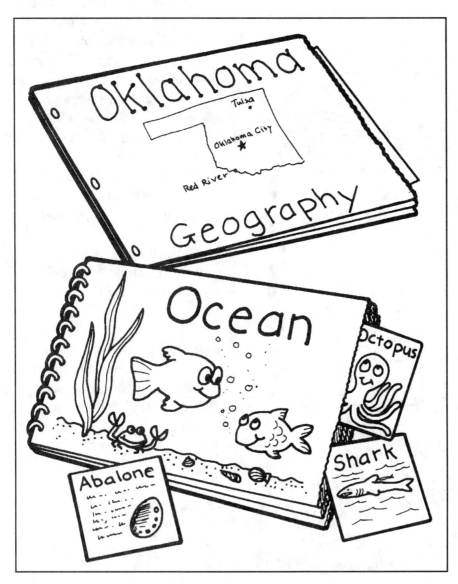

Box Projects

◆◆

Recycled boxes are perfect, inexpensive materials to use for student projects and center activities and for organizing classroom materials. Send home a note asking families to save specific boxes you might need, such as shoe boxes, pizza boxes, jewelry boxes, candy boxes, or gift boxes.

You can also purchase boxes at craft stores, stores that specialize in containers of all kinds, box companies, and paper companies. Here is a good source for buying boxes in larger quantities:

Xpedx paper store
1-800-351-8117

Basic supplies for box projects are listed on this page. Some projects call for additional materials. These are highlighted in the project descriptions.

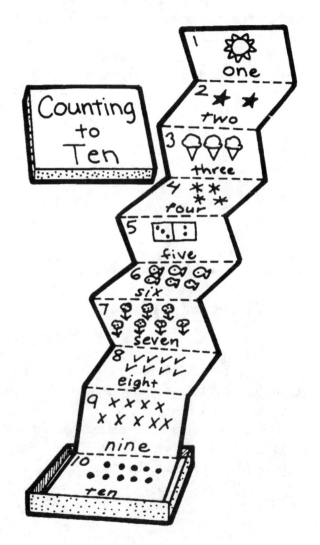

◆◆

Basic Supplies for Box Projects
- boxes, various sizes
- construction paper
- writing paper
- crayons, markers, colored pencils
- scissors
- glue
- tape

◆ "Getting to Know You" Box

Use this activity at the beginning of the year to help classmates get to know each other. Have students decorate their boxes with drawings or **magazine pictures** that represent things about themselves such as hobbies, family, pets, and favorite foods. Ask them to add a self-portrait "popping" out of the box. Children can use the boxes as props to share about themselves, or they can place them on their desks for Back-to-School Night.

◆ Bug Box

Read aloud *How Many Bugs in a Box?*, a delightful pop-up, counting book by David Carter. Have each student draw, cut, and glue bugs inside a box. Place all the bug boxes at a center. Students can count the bugs in each box, place the boxes in numerical order, or practice "asking and telling" sentences as modeled in the story. (E.g., How many bugs are in the small box? There are six tiny bugs.)

◆ Fraction Box

Ask students to save pizza boxes, or request donations from a local restaurant. Working in small groups, have students make paper pizzas, cut them into fractional parts, and label the parts. Place the fraction boxes at a math center, or use them for small group instruction on fractions. *Eating Fractions* by Bruce McMillan is the perfect book to use to introduce this activity.

◆ Books in a Box

Books in a Box are fun to make and fun to read. Use **adding machine tape** for small boxes, or trim **shelf paper** for larger boxes. Students can also tape together sheets of paper that are cut to fit the box. Have them accordion-fold the paper first; then write and illustrate the story. Show students how to glue the last page in the bottom of the box. Ask them to decorate the box lid like a book cover with title, author, and illustration.

◆ Riddle Box

Have students place a picture or object inside a box. Show them how to cut and glue on paper to fit the lid, and ask them to write a riddle about what is in the box. Label each box with a different number, and place them in a center. Give students numbered recording sheets to write their answers to the riddles. Or, have each child present his or her riddle box to the class.

I am red.
I am round.
I grow on trees.
I am a house for a worm.
What Am I ?

◆ Turtle Box

Give each child a box. Have students cut four legs, a head, and a tail out of green construction paper or **felt** and glue them to the bottom of the box. Ask them to color the top of the box with crayons or markers to look like a turtle shell. Students can write turtle facts or creative stories and place them inside the box.

The only reptile with a shell.

Turtles are cold-blooded.

Turtles have no teeth.

◆ Sequence Box

Sequence Boxes are constructed just like Books in a Box on page 45. Have students accordion-fold paper to fit their boxes. On the paper, ask them to write and/or illustrate any sequence of events such as a biographical or historical time line, a life cycle, or a set of directions. Have them glue the paper in the box and decorate the box cover appropriately.

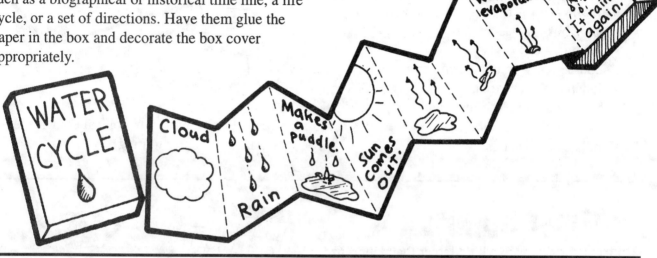

◆ Food Box

Ask students to bring in empty food boxes such as cereal, cookie, gelatin, and rice boxes. Cut up the boxes, and have students use the front and back surfaces as covers for books to go with a nutrition unit. For example, make a class ABC book using an alphabet cereal box. Or, use a Cheerios box for a book about circles. Spiral-bind the books, or punch holes and use yarn, rings, or paper fasteners.

◆ Bounty of Boxes

Use a variety of interesting boxes for storing theme-related curriculum materials. The following boxes and units are a good match:

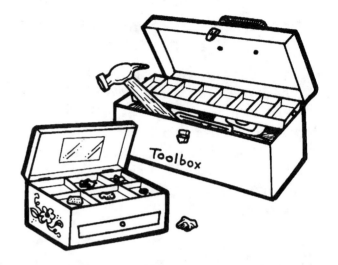

- toolbox – simple machines, measurement
- jewelry box – rocks, gems, minerals
- shoe box – measurement
- hat box – careers
- cookie box – fractions, cooking
- lunch box – nutrition
- tackle box – fish, lakes, ponds, streams
- candy box – math topics
- music box – songs
- cereal box – nutrition, consumer awareness
- mail box – letter writing

◆ Graphing Box

Collect boxes that are a little larger than letter-size paper. Laminate and tape a graphing grid inside the lid of the box. In the box, place **recording sheets** and **objects or pictures for students to graph**. Place this self-contained graphing activity at a math center. Change the objects frequently to vary graphing opportunities.

◆ Chalkboard Box

Purchase **chalkboard spray paint** (available in craft stores), and paint the lids of sturdy boxes. Students can store chalk and erasers inside the boxes and use these individual, mobile chalkboards for a wide variety of activities. You can also have students keep practice activities in their boxes (e.g., spelling words, math facts, handwriting).

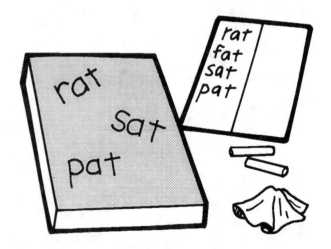

Flip-Flaps

Flip-flaps are instant projects that students can make and use with any area of the curriculum. Although flip-flaps have been around for a long time, the following pages will show you a wealth of unique variations on the flip-flap idea. For example, they can have two flaps or ten flaps; the fold can be at the top, at the bottom, or on the side; and extra pages can be added.

When selecting paper for flip-flaps, consider the amount of writing and illustrating students will be doing. Letter- or ledger-size (11" x 17") copy paper works well, as does construction paper (9" x 12" or 12" x 18"). A flip-flap that focuses on just two initial consonant sounds can be made from letter-size copy paper. A weeklong journal with seven flaps needs to be larger. For group projects, have students make large flip-flaps from butcher paper or chart paper.

Teach students how to make flip-flaps in small groups. Show them how to fold the paper lengthwise and then fold according to the number of flaps desired. Remind them to open the paper and cut the flaps only to the center fold. The back "page" should have no cuts. Basic supplies for flip-flap projects are listed on this page. A few projects call for additional materials. These are highlighted in the project description.

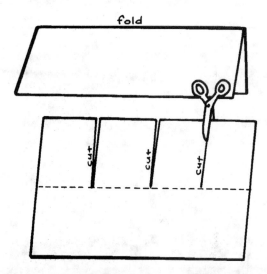

To add more pages, have students fold and cut two or three sheets of paper at one time. Then staple each flap on the fold so the pages will not slip out.

◆◆◆◆◆◆◆◆◆◆◆◆◆◆◆◆◆◆◆◆◆◆◆◆◆◆◆◆◆

Basic Supplies for Flip-Flap Projects
• unlined paper, various sizes
• crayons, markers, colored pencils
• scissors
• glue
• tape

◆ Compound Words

Have students write and illustrate two words on the front and the compound word under the flaps.

◆ Cause and Effect

When learning about cause and effect, have students record examples from stories they have read.

◆ Letter Sounds

Use flip-flaps to reinforce phonics skills. Tell students which letters to write on the flaps. Then ask them to write words and/or draw pictures of words that begin with the letter sounds. Send this flip-flap for homework, and ask students to cut out **magazine pictures** to glue inside.

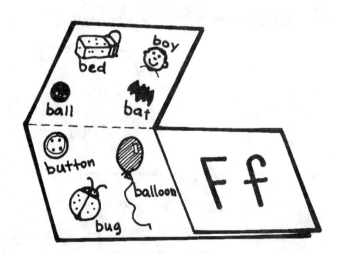

◆ Characters, Setting, Plot

Use this flip-flap as a rough draft format for original stories. Students can draw and/or write ideas for the characters, setting, and plot under the flaps.

◆ KWL

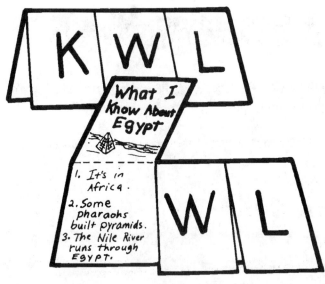

Use K (what I know), W (what I want to know), L (what I learned) when introducing a new theme or unit of study. Have children fill in the K and W part before the unit and the L part when the study is completed. This will work for any area of the curriculum.

◆ Three Little Pigs

Read aloud *The Three Little Pigs*; then use this flip-flap for story retelling. With the fold on the bottom, have students cut each flap to a point to make a roof. Ask them to color the houses to represent the straw, stick, and brick pig houses. They can draw the pigs inside each house.

◆ Venn Diagrams

Compare two animals, stories, characters, famous people, and so on with this flip-flap. Show students how to use a Venn diagram-type format. For example, read aloud the *Frog and Toad* books by Arnold Lobel. Then have students list Frog's unique traits under the first flap, Toad's traits under the last flap, and traits they have in common under the center flap.

◆ Beginning, Middle, End

Have students use this flip-flap to develop a rough draft of an original story. Or, ask them to record the sequence of events for a book they have read.

◆ Character, Setting, Problem, Solution

Ask students to record the main characters, setting, problem, and solution for a story they have read.

◆ Opposites

Ask students to write one word and illustrate it on the front. They can write and illustrate the opposite word on the inside.

◆ Rhyming Words

Dictate words for students to write and illustrate on the front. Have them write and illustrate rhyming words inside. Show students how to add extra "pages" so they can write several rhyming words. (See page 49 for directions.) They can use the rhyming words to write a poem.

◆ New Ending

Ask students to label the flaps as follows: *Character, Setting, Problem, Solution, New Ending*. Have them respond to a book they have heard or read and write a new ending under the last flap.

◆ Classroom Journal

With the fold on the left, ask students to label Monday through Friday on the front. Under each flap, have them write a journal entry for that day.

◆ Homework Journal

Have students cut seven flaps and label with the days of the week. Ask them to keep the journal at home for a week and write an entry for each day.

◆ Days of the Week

Cookie's Week by Cindy Ward is the story of a cat who gets into a different kind of mischief each day of the week. Have children write similar stories using the days-of-the-week pattern. Ask them to cut seven flaps, label the flaps as shown, and write about the mischievous animal events inside.

◆ Story Problems

Write one math problem on the front of each flap.
On the inside, ask students to write and illustrate
story problems that match the number sentences
on the front. Answers can go on the back.

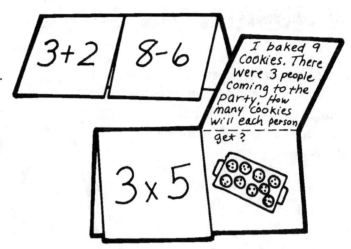

◆ Fact Families

Have students write the number for a fact family on
the front of the flap and record the facts under the
flap.

◆ Shapes

Have students draw shapes on the front and
then draw several classroom objects that are
the same shape under each flap. For homework,
have students cut and paste pictures inside.

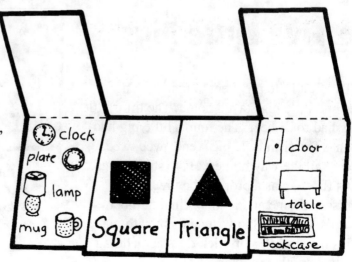

◆ Number Words

Use construction paper for this flip-flap. Have students write numerals and glue an appropriate number of **beans** on each flap. Ask them to write and illustrate the number words inside.

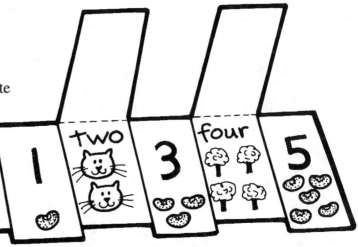

◆ Five Little Pumpkins

Have students cut five flaps. With the fold at the bottom, show them how to cut points at the top to make a fence. Ask them to draw the slats and color them brown. Have them write and illustrate one stanza of the poem "Five Little Pumpkins" (page 112) inside each flap. (They will have to write the first stanza on the front of the first flap.)

◆ Five Little Pigs

"The first little pig went to market. The second little pig stayed home. The third little pig had roast beef. The fourth little pig had none. The fifth little pig went, 'wee, wee, wee,' all the way home." Have students use this flip-flap as a prop as they recite the nursery rhyme and learn ordinal number words. Option: Show students how to make pigs using **pink self-stick dots** and adding features with a marker.

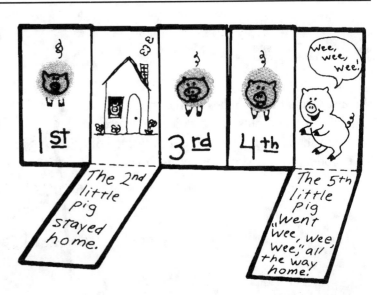

◆ Sink and Float

Ask students to record observations about a simple science experiment. Younger students can draw pictures of which objects sink or float. Older children can record predictions and observations about the experiment.

◆ Head, Thorax, Abdomen

During an insect unit, have students label the three flaps *Head, Thorax,* and *Abdomen.* Ask them to illustrate the three main body parts inside.

◆ Solids, Liquids, Gases

Have students draw examples of solids, liquids, and gases under the correct flaps.

◆ Plants

With the fold on the left, have students label the flaps *leaf, stem*, and *root*. They can draw and/or write about the parts inside.

◆ Seasons

Have students label each flap with the name of a season and use the inside to show what a tree looks like in winter, spring, summer, and fall. Or, ask students to list seasonal activities, months, or holidays under the correct season.

◆ Rain Forest

With the fold on the left, have students draw the layers of the rain forest inside and label the flaps *Forest Floor, Understory, Canopy,* and *Emergent Layer.* Ask them to write about each layer inside.

◆ Inside the Earth

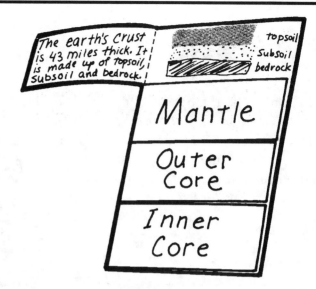

With the fold on the left, ask students to label the flaps *Crust, Mantle, Outer Core*, and *Inner Core*. On the inside, they can write facts about the corresponding layers of the earth.

◆ Life Cycle

Invite students to record life-cycle stages in this flip-flap. For example, for an insect unit, have them label the flaps *Egg, Larva, Pupa,* and *Adult* and draw or tell about each stage inside.

◆ Animal Classifications

Have the children write animal classifications on the flaps. Ask them to write and illustrate one example for each classification inside, naming distinguishing characteristics.

◆ Five Senses

Have students label the flaps as follows: *I See, I Hear, I Taste, I Smell,* and *I Touch.* Ask them to write and illustrate facts about each of the five senses inside. Or, they can list descriptive words under each flap such as *sweet, spicy, sour,* and *salty* under *I Taste.*

◆ Dirt

With the fold on the left, ask students to label the flaps *Humus, Clay, Silt, Sand,* and *Gravel.* Have them write about each soil layer on the inside.

◆ Planets

Give students ledger-size paper. Have them cut nine flaps, write the name of one planet on each flap, and write and illustrate facts about the planets inside.

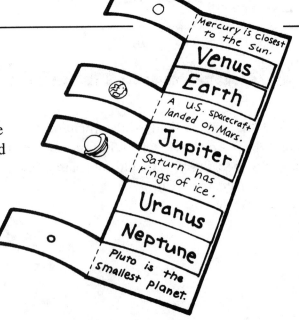

◆ Air, Land, Sea

With the fold on the left, ask students to label the flaps *In the Air, On the Land,* and *In the Water.* Have them draw modes of transportation under the flaps.

◆ States

Have students label the first flap with the name of a state. Ask them to label the other flaps *State Bird, State Flower,* and *State Rock.* On the inside, ask them to write and illustrate information about the state.

◆ Who, What, When, Where, Why

Invite students to use this flip-flap for a mini-report on a famous person. Have them label the flaps *Who, What, When, Where,* and *Why* and fill in the information inside. This flip-flap can also be used as a rough draft outline for a story.

◆ Geography

Have students write geographical terms on the front and define and illustrate the terms inside. The number of flaps will vary.

◆ Time Line

Invite students to make a time line of important events in their lives (or a famous person's life). Have them label each flap with a year or a certain time period. They can list and illustrate important events on the inside. The number of flaps will vary.

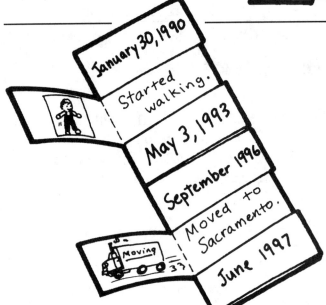

◆ Continent Review

Ask students to cut seven flaps and write the names of the continents on the flaps. Have them write facts about each continent inside.

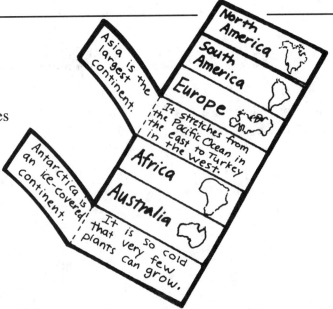

Slit Books

Slit books are especially versatile because the number of pages can be increased or decreased to fit the writing project. You will need two sheets of paper for an eight-page book, three sheets for a twelve-page book, and so on. Basic supplies for making slit books are listed on this page. Some projects call for additional materials. These are highlighted in the project descriptions.

The instructions for making a basic slit book are shown below, but there are some special considerations for making a slit book that has a particular shape. Be sure to cut out the shape *before* making the cuts shown in steps 2 and 3. Cut all pages at the same time so they will have the exact same shape. The fold can be on the left, top, or bottom, depending on the shape of the book.

1. Fold the sheets of paper in half as shown. If you are making a shape slit book, cut the basic shape now.

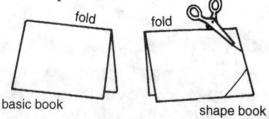

basic book   shape book

2. Open *one* of the folded sheets and bend it in half lengthwise. (Do not crease it.) Cut on the fold line from the bend to within 1" of the edge of the paper. One-half of this page will serve as the cover.

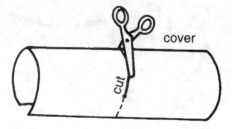

cover

cut

3. Take the remaining sheets of paper and cut in 1" from each edge on the fold as shown.

4. Bend the book pages in half lengthwise and slide them through the long slit in the cover.

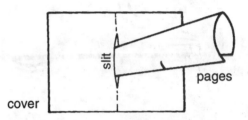

slit

pages

cover

5. Ease open the pages until they fit into the slit.

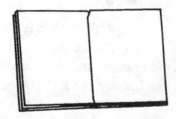

6. Decorate the cover, and write and illustrate on the inside pages.

colors

Basic Supplies for Slit Books
* unlined paper, various sizes
* crayons, markers, colored pencils
* scissors

◆ Mouse

Keeping the fold at the bottom, have students cut the pages into a mouse shape. Provide yarn for the tail. Invite students to use this book for writing activities centered around a mouse theme. Some related book titles are: *Frederick* by Leo Lionni, *Owen* by Kevin Henkes, and *Mouse Paint* by Ellen Stoll Walsh.

Frederick is a daydreamer and poet. Instead of gathering food, he collects "colors" for a gray winter's day.

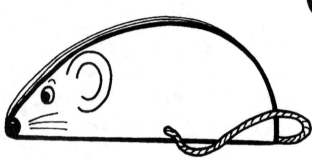

◆ Rabbit

A pattern for the rabbit slit book is included on page 110. The fold is at the bottom. Have students draw in rabbit features and glue on **cotton ball** tails. They can use this book to respond to fictional rabbit stories, write their own stories, or record facts about rabbits.

Rabbits come in all sizes. The Flemish giant rabbit can weigh 15 to 16 pounds.

◆ School Bus

To make a long bus, have students fold the paper lengthwise and then round off the top corners. The fold is at the top. They can add construction paper wheels and draw people on the bus. Use this slit book when it's time for a field trip. Ask students to record field trip notes and observations and evaluate the trip on the last page.

◆ Butterfly

A pattern for the butterfly slit book is included on page 111. The fold is at the bottom. Have students use this book to record the life cycle of a butterfly or write facts about a specific butterfly or moth. The cover can be decorated to match the wing pattern. Consider making a large version of the book so students can make a class book. Read *The Butterfly Alphabet Book* by Brian Cassiet and Jerry Pallotta to introduce this activity.

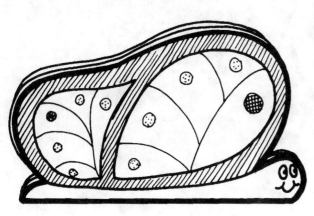

◆ Pyramid

With the fold at the bottom, have students cut a triangular shape. Use this book when studying about Egypt, or use it along with a nutrition unit. Read aloud *The Edible Pyramid* by Loreen Leedy; then have students illustrate a nutritious breakfast, lunch, or dinner inside.

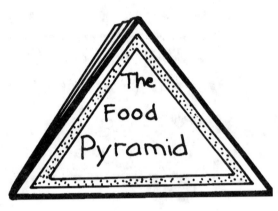

◆ Heart

With the fold on the left, have students cut half a heart shape. They can embellish the cover with **glitter, lace**, and **ribbon**. Invite students to write Valentine poems and riddles inside.

◆ Watermelon

With the fold at the top, have students round off the bottom corners to make a watermelon shape. After coloring, they can glue on real **seeds**. Have students use this book to record watermelon estimation activities, keep a gardening journal, or write about summer activities.

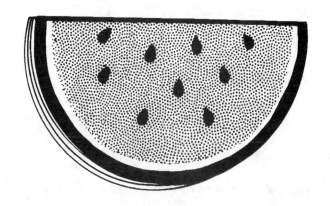

◆ Baseball Cap

This shape is cut with the fold on the bottom. Students can use this book for sports theme activities. Or have them follow the progress of a favorite baseball team. They can record wins, losses, player statistics, and so on.

◆ Top Hat

This slit book is perfect for a study of Abraham Lincoln. Children can use the book to write facts, quotes, or poems about Honest Abe. The fold can be at the top or bottom.

◆ Cowboy Hat

Cowboys used their hats for more than just protection. Have children research the many uses for a cowboy hat and record them in this book. They can also record cowboy vocabulary or journal entries telling about a day in the life of a cowboy.

◆ Turtle

Have students hold the fold at the bottom and cut a turtle shape. They can add construction paper legs and tails. Use this book with a science unit on turtles or pond life. Or read the series of *Franklin* books by Paulette Bourgeois, and have students write new endings for Franklin's adventures.

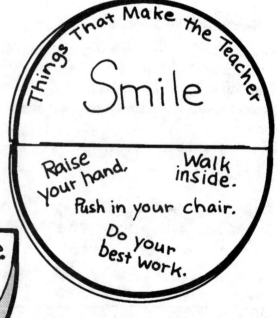

◆ Smile

Use this book to start the school year off with a smile. Ask students to list things that make them smile, things they can do to make each other smile, and things they can do to make the teacher smile. Or have students make mini joke books for class-mates to read. The fold is at the top in this book.

◆ Domino

There is no special cutting for the domino slit book. The fold is on the left. Read aloud *Domino Addition* by Lynette Long, a book that uses dominoes to illustrate simple addition. Have students use real dominoes as manipulatives and then write fact families in the domino book. Ask them to draw a domino on the left-hand page and write the fact family on the right-hand page.

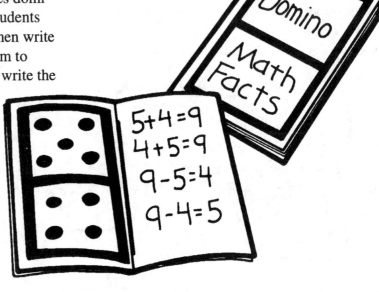

◆ Caterpillar

Have students fold paper lengthwise; then round off the corners. The fold can be at the top or bottom. Read aloud *The Very Hungry Caterpillar* by Eric Carle. Have students write their own versions of the story inside the caterpillar book. Or pair this book with the butterfly slit book (page 65) during a unit on insects.

◆ Pencil

Have students cut a point at one end and round off the other end to make a pencil shape. The fold can be at the top or bottom. This book can be used all year long. Have students list possible writing topics, write journal entries, record punctuation rules, or make dictionaries on any topic.

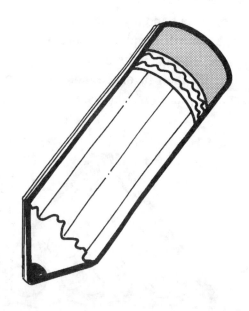

Things I want to write about:
1. Trip to Washington, D.C.
2. My birthday party.
3. Sleepover at Kim's house.
4. What I learned about my hermit crab.
5. My soccer team not winning this weekend.

◆ Window

Have students make a basic slit book and decorate the window with curtains, drapes, or a shade. They can also add objects or people in the window. Have students use the book for descriptive writing activities. For example, they can cut scenes from magazines, travel brochures, or scenic calendars to glue on the left-hand pages. Ask them to write descriptions on the right-hand pages.

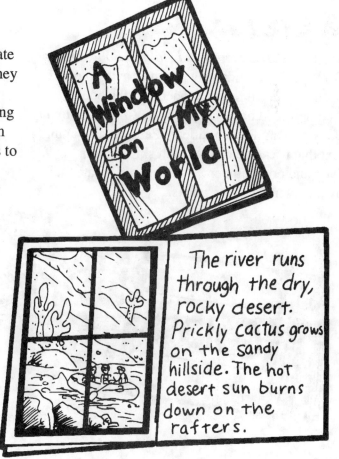

A Window on My World

The river runs through the dry, rocky desert. Prickly cactus grows on the sandy hillside. The hot desert sun burns down on the rafters.

◆ Pizza

Have students cut and decorate a large triangular shape. The crust of the pizza should be on the fold. Inside, have students write directions for making a pizza, describe their favorite kind of pizza, or add up the cost of pizza ingredients.

◆ Crayon

Read aloud *Hailstones and Halibut Bones* by Mary O'Neill. Have students write their own color poems modeled after the poems in the book. Another good book to use is *The Crayon Counting Book* by Pam Ryan and Jerry Pallotta, a rhyming text that uses crayons to teach skip counting by even and odd numbers. Students can create their own crayon counting books.

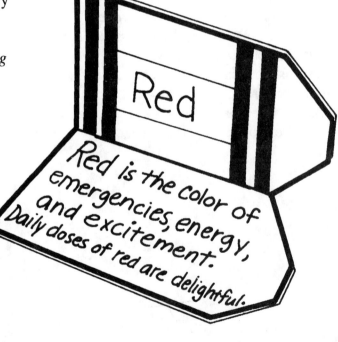

Poof Books

The poof book is made from one sheet of paper and can be used for a wide variety of writing activities. A sheet of 8-1/2" x 11" paper makes a small book (2-3/4" x 4-1/4"), so you may want to use larger sheets for bigger books. Basic supplies for making poof books are listed on this page. But it's also fun to make them with other materials such as wrapping paper and newspaper. These materials are highlighted in the project descriptions.

Following the directions below, show small groups of students how to make a basic book. After a few times, students will be able to make this book in less than a minute. Introduce the variations described on the following pages when they fit in with your curriculum.

1. Fold the paper in half width-wise. Then fold it once more in the same direction.

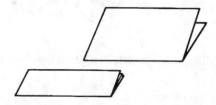

2. Fold the paper in half in the opposite direction.

3. Open to a half sheet. Starting from the folded edge, cut along the crease. Stop where the fold lines intersect.

4. Open the paper completely.

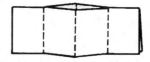

5. Fold the paper lengthwise.

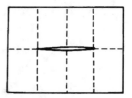

6. Grasp the outer edges as shown and push them towards the center. The opening should "poof" out. Keep pushing until a book of four sections is formed.

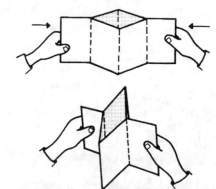

7. Fold the pages closed. Write the title on the cover.

Basic Supplies for Poof Books
- unlined paper, various sizes
- scissors
- markers, crayons, colored pencils
- glue
- construction paper

◆ More Pages

The original poof book has a cover and six pages. If you need a seven-page book, use the back cover as a page. Seven-page books are handy for days-of-the-week activities. For longer books, have students place two or three poof books inside each other and slip a heavy rubber band around the middle. This is a handy way to make individual alphabet books for use with any area of the curriculum.

For a permanent binding, help students **hole-punch** the book at the top and bottom of the spine and tie the book together with **ribbon**, **yarn**, or **string**.

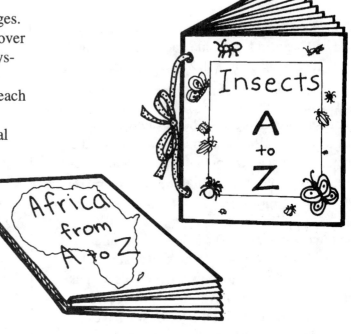

◆ Wrapping Paper

Ask parents to collect and save **wrapping paper** for the publishing center in your classroom. Cut the paper into sheets, whatever size you choose, and have students follow the basic poof book directions. They will need to glue white paper on the inside pages. Two suggestions for activities include having students use a wild animal pattern for books on endangered animals or a birthday pattern for writing about their favorite birthday party.

◆ Newspaper

Recycle **newspaper** into poof books. Give each student a full sheet of newspaper. Have them follow the basic poof book directions. They will need to glue white paper on the inside pages for writing and illustrating. Have the students use the comics to make joke books and use the sports section to write sports stories.

◆ Butcher Paper

Make big books with large sheets of **butcher paper** following the basic poof book directions. Have students write original versions of familiar poems, chants, stories, or songs.

◆ Paper Bags

Reuse **paper bags** to make poof books. First, create a single rectangular sheet by cutting down one fold line and then cutting off the bottom of the bag. Have students follow the basic instructions to make the book and use markers to write and draw on the brown pages.

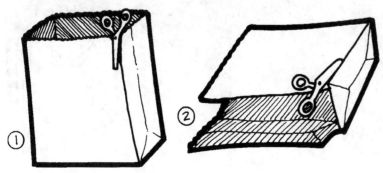

◆ Shape Poof Books

Students can cut a basic poof book into a special shape to fit a particular topic. It's best to keep the shape very simple. Caution them not to cut completely around the edge, because the book will fall apart. Shape big books made out of colored **butcher paper** are the best!

◆ Button
Round off the corners and add two or four holes

◆ Apple
Make an apple out of red butcher paper, and add a construction paper stem and leaves.

◆ Water
Cut waves at the top of a book made out of blue paper.

◆ Pocket
Cut off the corners at the bottom, and add stitching around the edge.

◆ Pumpkin
Using orange paper, round off the top and bottom, and add a stem.

◆ Frog and Toad
Use green or brown butcher paper, and add construction paper eyes.

Tri-Fold Books

This simple book will become a favorite for both you and your students. It's easy to make, and the variations are endless. Change the size of the book according to the writing activity. Standard letter-size copy paper is fine for small tri-fold books. Full sheets (12" x 18") of construction paper allow more room for text and illustrations. Use large sheets of butcher paper or chart paper to make tri-fold big books.

Show small groups of children how to make tri-fold books. First teach them how to fold the paper into three equal parts. If the book is a special shape, show them how to lightly outline and then cut out the shape. Caution students about leaving some of the paper connected at the folds, the same as in cutting out paper dolls. You may want to provide simple patterns for young students. Two patterns are provided on pages 108-109.

1. Fold

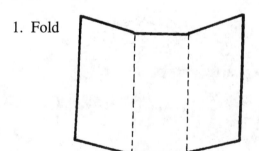

2. Cut   3. Decorate

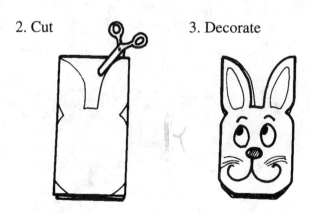

Basic supplies for tri-fold books are listed on this page. Some projects call for additional materials. These are highlighted in the project descriptions.

◆◆◆◆◆◆◆◆◆◆◆◆◆◆◆◆◆◆◆◆◆◆◆◆

Basic Supplies for Tri-Fold Books
- unlined paper
- construction paper, various sizes
- crayons, markers, colored pencils
- scissors
- glue
- tape

◆ Snowball

Show students how to round off the corners to cut a snowball shape. They can write words beginning with the "sn" blend, a recipe for snow ice cream, or rules for a snowball fight. Older students can write about the properties of snow.

◆ Cloud

The cloud tri-fold opens vertically. Students can glue **cotton** to the front and use the inside to illustrate different kinds of clouds. Or, read aloud *It Looked Like Spilt Milk* by Charles G. Shaw as a model for writing. This book shows how clouds often resemble real objects. Have students make the cloud book out of blue paper, tear white paper into three different shapes, and glue the shapes in the book. Ask them to use the pattern in the story to write their own books.

◆ Button

Have students cut a button shape and use this book for a variety of button activities. They can sort buttons into three groups and record how they sorted. Or have them make and record three different button patterns inside.

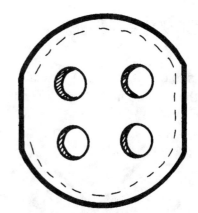

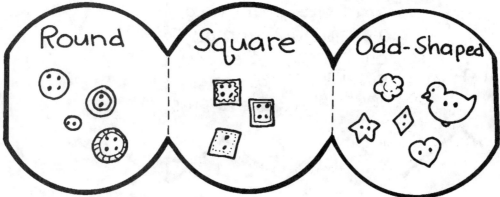

◆ Soup Bowl

Alphabet pasta is a perfect addition to a spelling center. Have children spell words with pasta or magnetic letters and then write them inside the soup bowl book. Then they can write the title and glue alphabet pasta on the front. Celebrate National Soup Month in January by having the children take the book home and copy a favorite family soup recipe. End the month with a soup-tasting party!

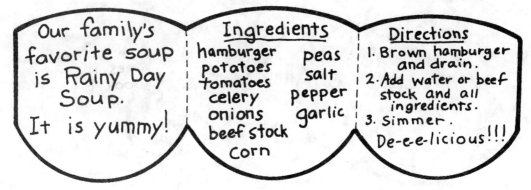

◆ Rocket Ship

Ask students to choose a planet, research it, and write what they would need to pack for a visit to the planet.

◆ Snowman

A pattern for this book is provided on page 109. Have students draw snowman features or use **collage items** such as buttons and fabric. On the inside, they can write a snowman story, list different kinds of winter activities, or write directions for making a snowman.

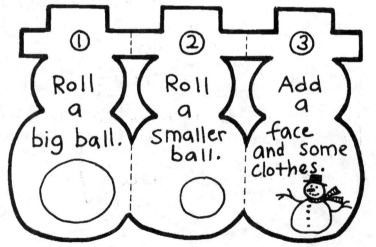

◆ Tree

Use this book for a variety of nature activities and themes: birds, trees, woodland animals, ecology. Have students use green paper for the tri-fold part, which is cut like the snowball on page 78. Ask them to cut a trunk out of brown poster board and glue it on. They can add **twigs** for a more natural look and **animal stickers** to show animals that live in trees. Read aloud *A Tree Is Nice* by Janice Udry. Have students write their own reasons why a tree is nice.

◆ Candy

Have students cut a candy shape as shown. Invite them to sort and graph different kinds of candy. Ask them to write about the experience inside the book. Or use the candy book for thank-you notes.

◆ Birthday Cake

Use large sheets of construction paper to make a tri-fold birthday cake for each child. When each child celebrates his or her birthday, have classmates sign the card. Let the birthday child add the correct number of **tagboard** candles. Celebrate summer birthdays as half-birthdays.

◆ Ice-Cream Cone

A pattern for this book is provided on page 108. Have students invent a new flavor of ice cream, write about their favorite ice-cream flavor, or write an ice-cream poem.

◆ Carrot

Provide orange paper for this book. Have students cut a carrot shape. Then show them how to trace and cut around one hand on green paper to make the top. Have students write about healthy foods or gardening experiences in their books. Ask them to write about the beginning, middle, and end of related books such as *The Tale of Peter Rabbit* by Beatrix Potter or *The Carrot Seed* by Ruth Krauss.

◆ Peanut

In this book, have students record information from activities such as growing peanut plants, making peanut butter, graphing, a peanut butter taste test, and George Washington Carver research. Provide tan paper, or have children color white paper, including the nuts inside.

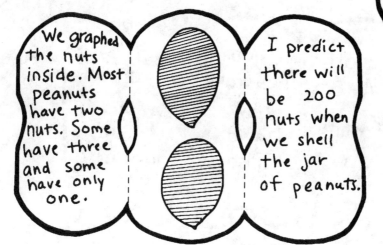

◆ Penguin

Have students cut the basic shape from black paper and add details as shown. Glue on **paper hole reinforcers** for eyes and an orange paper or **felt** beak. Use the book *Tacky the Penguin* by Helen Lester to motivate students to write make-believe penguin stories. Or ask children to write facts about real penguins. Students can write on white paper and glue it inside the book.

◆ Pig

Students can use the pig book to write a variation of the *Three Little Pigs*, list their favorite pig books, or write about their favorite pig character. Provide students with pink paper. Show them how to cut a spiral paper tail or to twist a **pipe cleaner** and tape it to the back.

◆ Cave

Provide gray or tan paper for the cave book. Have students round off the top and draw rocks and an opening. Students can write long *a* words inside the cave or use this book when studying bats, bears, or hibernation.

◆ Fish

Read *The Rainbow Fish* by Marcus Pfister, a story of how the most beautiful fish in the ocean discovers the real value of personal beauty and friendship. Students can decorate a tri-fold fish book with **tissue paper, bright wrapping paper, sequins,** and **glitter** to make their own rainbow fish. Inside, have them list qualities of a good friend.

◆ Rabbit

Students can write rabbit facts or make-believe rabbit stories in the rabbit book. If you have a pet classroom rabbit, have students write observations or list instructions for proper pet care.

Our rabbit's name is Buffet. He is our class pet.

Sometimes he hops around in our room. We build mazes for him to hop in.

Buffet likes carrots and alfalfa. We clean his cage every week.

◆ Tooth

Have a supply of tooth tri-fold books on hand to pass out to students who have lost a tooth. They can record the date, tell about how the tooth came out, or write letters to the tooth fairy. The tooth book can also be used in February for Dental Health Month. Have students list ways to care for their teeth.

Take Care of Your Teeth

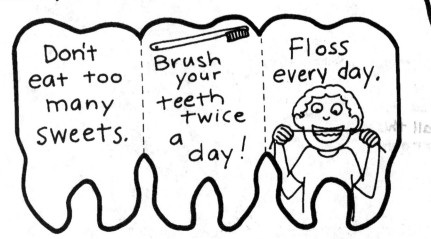

Don't eat too many sweets.

Brush your teeth twice a day!

Floss every day.

◆ Pillow

The pillow tri-fold opens vertically. Children can decorate the pillow and write about a favorite sleepover or tell about their sweet or scary dreams.

Sleepover at Joe's

I spent the night at Joe's house.

We made pizza and brownies.

We played a soccer game the next morning. We won! Joe scored!

◆ Spider

Provide black or brown paper for the spider book. Show students how to accordion-fold and tape four long strips to the back of the book for eight legs. They can add cut paper eyes (or **wiggly eyes**) and glue white paper on the inside. Ask children to write spider observations, tell about a particular spider, or write spider facts inside.

A spider crawled up the wall this afternoon.

It jumped to a branch and started to spin a web.

After dinner I saw a bug caught in the web. I guess the spider was hungry too!

◆ Bed

Have students decorate a bedspread or quilt on the front of the book with crayons, markers, or **fabric scraps**. Children can use the bed book to write about staying in bed when sick. They can tell about a magic bed taking them on an adventure, or they can write story problems based on the poem "No More Monkeys Jumping on the Bed."

◆ Whale

The whale tri-fold opens vertically. Have students cut a whale shape as shown. They can also color, cut, and tape a spout to the back of the book. Invite them to use the book for ocean theme activities.

Fold-Over Projects

Fold-overs are quick and easy to make. Use them to liven-up short writing assignments. Fold-overs are perfect for invitations and greeting cards. They also make attractive student work displays.

Following the directions below, show children how to make a basic fold-over project. Then demonstrate how to make shape fold-overs as shown on pages 90-95. Encourage students to come up with original fold-over designs to fit theme units or individual projects.

1. Fold a sheet of paper in half width-wise, and crease the fold.

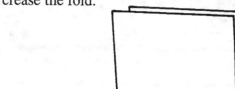

2. Take *one* top edge and fold it back down to the fold.

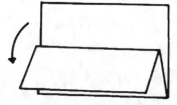

3. If you are making a shape fold-over, cut the shape now.

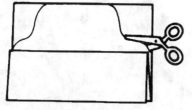

4. Illustrate the front. Write and/or draw on the inside.

Basic supplies for fold-over projects are listed on this page. Some projects call for additional materials. These are highlighted in the project descriptions.

For each of the activities that follow, start with the basic folding directions on this page.

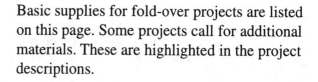

Basic Supplies for Fold-Over Projects
- unlined paper, various sizes
- crayons, markers, colored pencils
- scissors

◆ Foot

Have older children draw and cut out a foot shape. (You may want to prepare a pattern for younger students.) Ask them to label the fold-over *Put Your Best Foot Forward*. As a class, discuss the meaning of this familiar saying. Ask each student to describe an incident when they did their best.

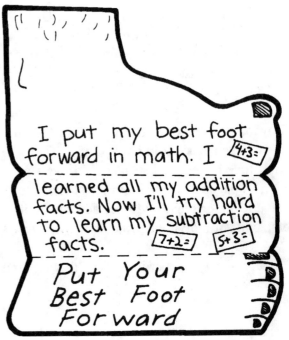

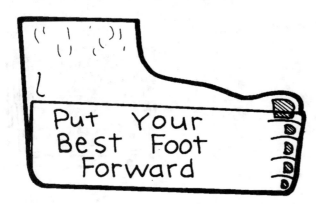

◆ Band-Aid

Show students how to round off all four corners to make a Band-Aid shape. Use pink paper for the traditional Band-Aid, or use white paper and have students make fancy band-aids. Introduce this project by reading aloud the poem "Band-Aids" from *Where the Sidewalk Ends* by Shel Silverstein. Have students write about times they have needed Band-Aids.

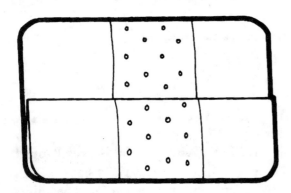

◆ Tree

Keeping the fold in a vertical position, have
students draw a tree on the front. On the inside,
ask them to list things that are made from trees,
animals that live in and around trees, or all the
benefits we get from trees. This fold-over is
perfect to use for Arbor Day or Earth Day
activities.

◆ Car

With the fold at the bottom, have students draw
and cut out a simple car shape. Or provide a
template for younger children to trace. Use this
fold-over with a transportation unit, or ask students
to describe a favorite car trip.

◆ Hamburger

Have students round off all four corners and color a delicious hamburger on the front. They can list their favorite hamburger ingredients, write the steps for making a hamburger, or describe a favorite BBQ party.

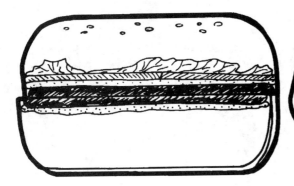

◆ My Head Is Full of . . .

Model for students how to make this fold-over so that the top of the head will "open up." With the fold at the top, have students draw the eyes, nose, and mouth below the center fold. Read aloud *My Head Is Full of Colors* by Catherine Friend. It's the story of Maria who wakes up each morning and finds her head full of colors, animals, books, and people. Ask students to write and illustrate what their heads are full of.

Teachin' Cheap

◆ Garden

Keeping the fold at the bottom, have students illustrate the above-ground parts of a garden on the front. Ask them to illustrate roots and underground animals such as ants, gophers, and worms on the inside.

◆ Present

With the fold at the bottom, have students draw a gift box, complete with bow and wrapping paper, on the front of the fold-over. Inside, ask them to answer one of these questions: What would you like for your birthday? What gift would you give your favorite book character? What gift would you give your best friend? What is the best gift you have ever received? Or have students use it to respond to books with a birthday theme such as *Mr. Rabbit and the Lovely Present* by Charlotte Zolotow.

◆ Balloon

Have students color a balloon on the front. The fold can be at the top or bottom. *Balloon Science* by Etta Kaner has 50 experiments and activities to do with balloons. Try some of the investigations, and have students record their observations and findings. Or read aloud *The Blue Balloon* by Mick Inkpen, the story of a boy and his magical balloon. Invite students to write about a balloon with strange and wonderful powers.

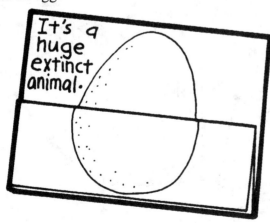

◆ Egg

As you read aloud *Egg!* by A.J. Wood, students will discover what creatures hatch out of different kinds of eggs. Ask students to draw an egg on the front and draw and write about the animal inside. Or have them write about an imaginary animal hatching out of an egg.

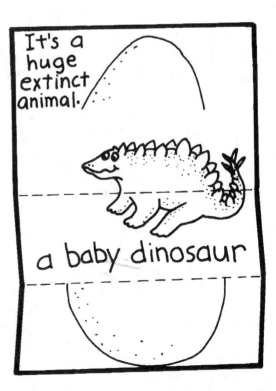

◆ Covered Wagon

Use this fold-over as part of a western movement unit. Keeping the fold in a vertical position, have students draw a covered wagon on the front. On the inside, they can list provisions needed for the journey or draw a map of their route west.

◆ Continents

Give students small continental maps. Have them cut the maps in half and glue the halves on the front of the fold-over. Ask them to write facts about the continent on the inside.

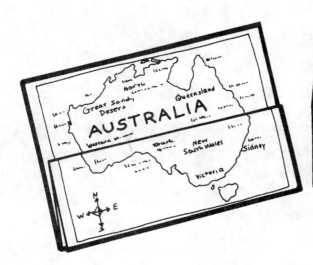

Notes

 Creative Teaching Press

Teachin' Cheap

Reproducibles

Apple   # Pumpkin

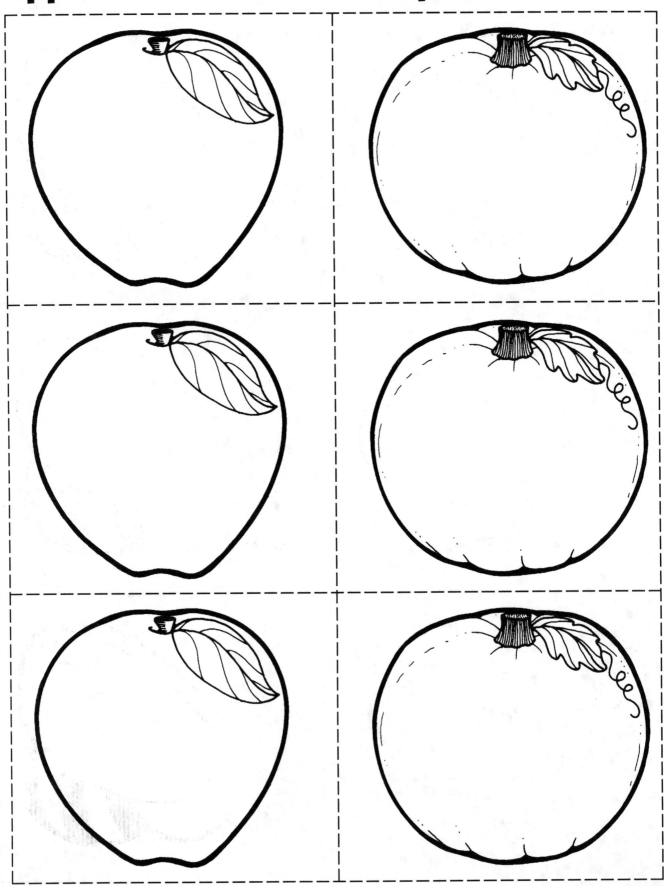

Teachin' Cheap

Ant   # Bee

Ladybug   # Fly

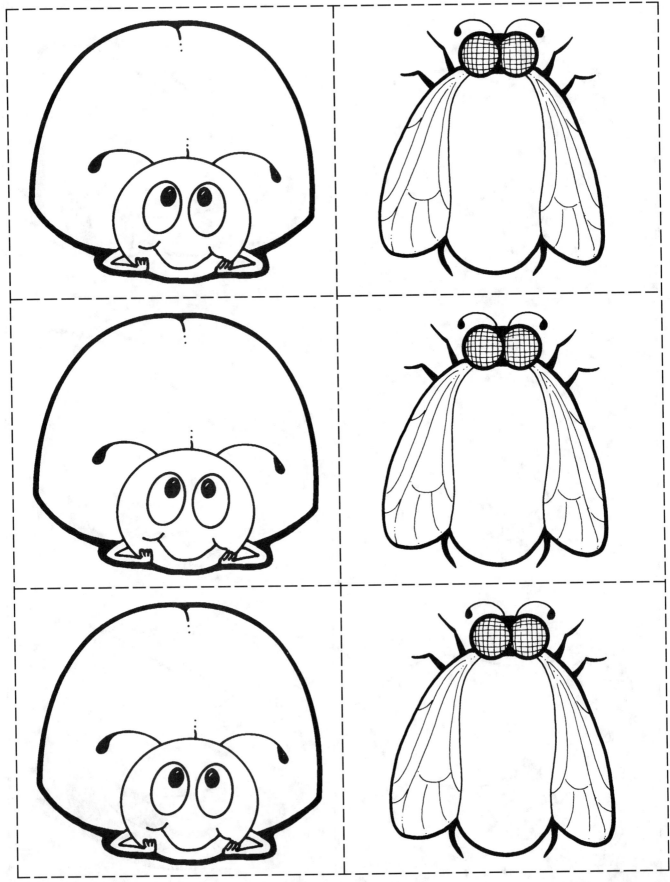

Teachin' Cheap

Flower

Sun

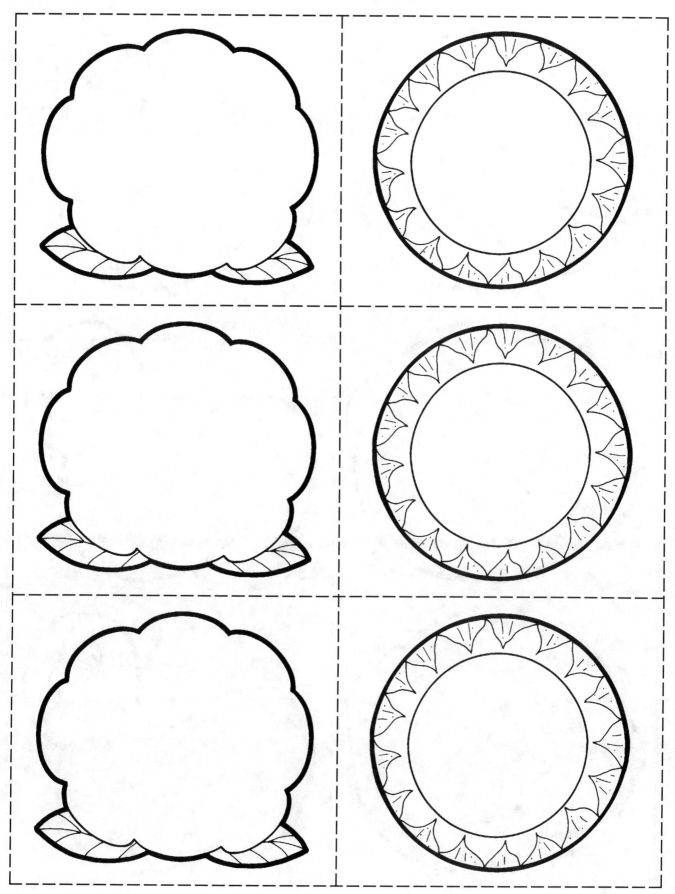

Rock

Worm

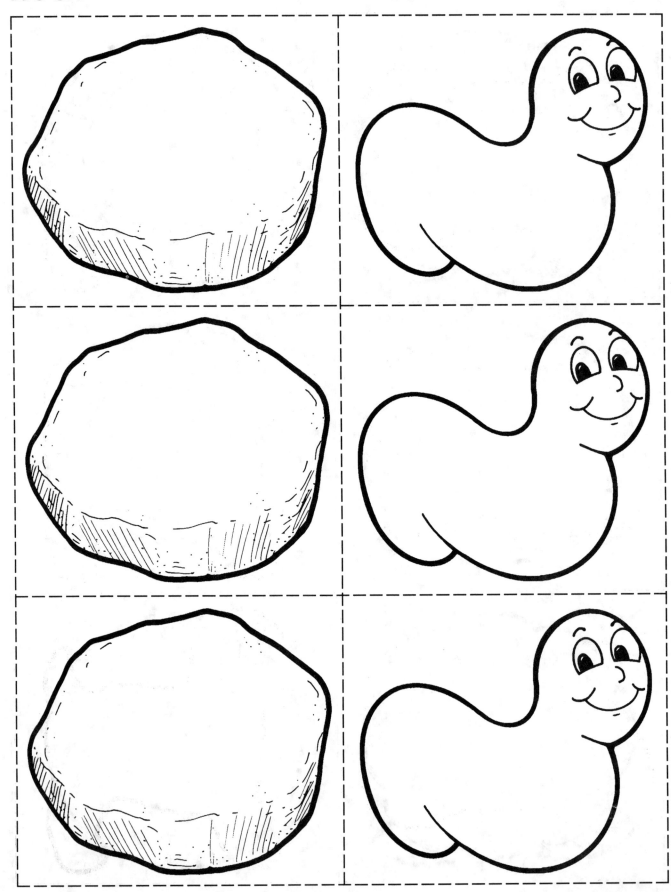

Bone

Dog

Pig

Cow

Bat

Bear

Mouse

Peanut

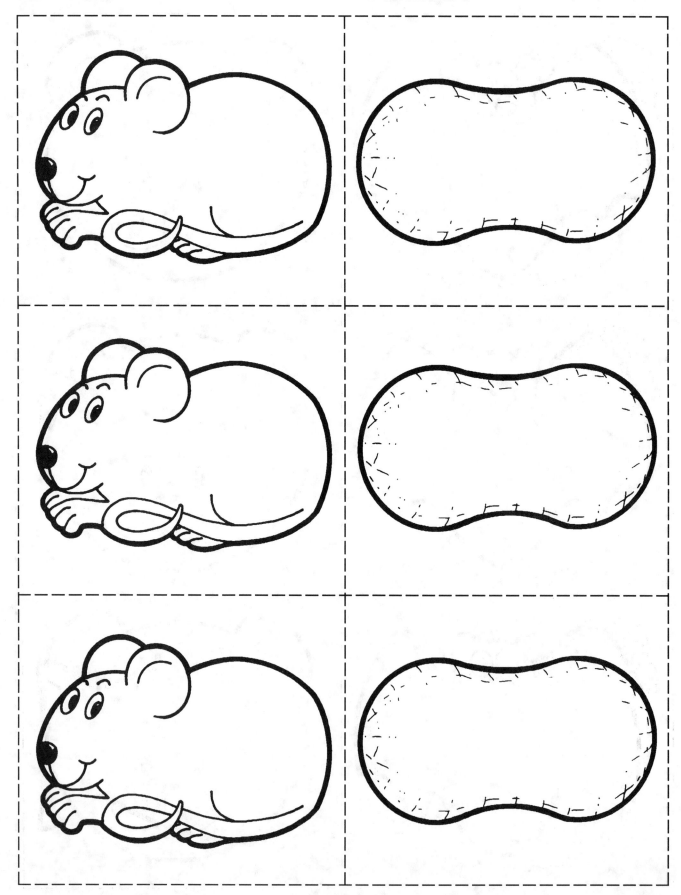

Chicken

Fish

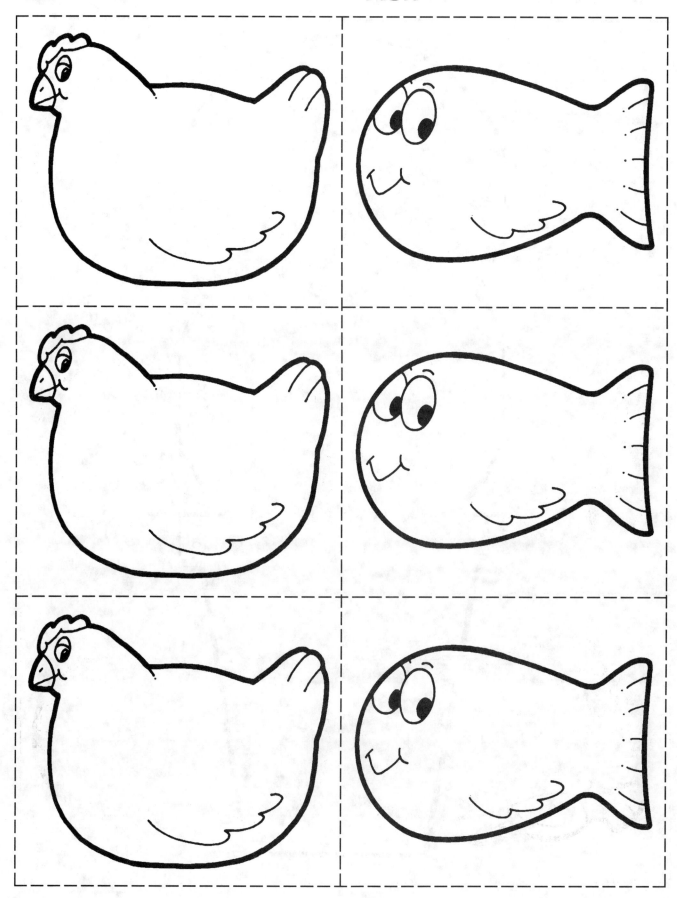

Ice-Cream Cone (Tri-Fold Book)

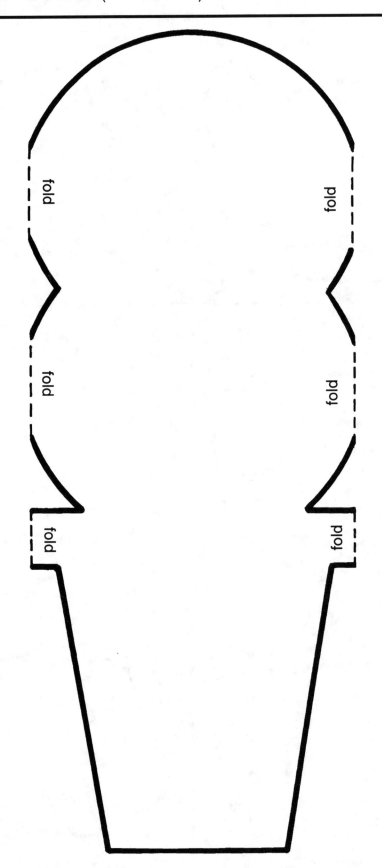

fold

fold

fold

fold

fold

fold

Snowman (Tri-Fold Book)

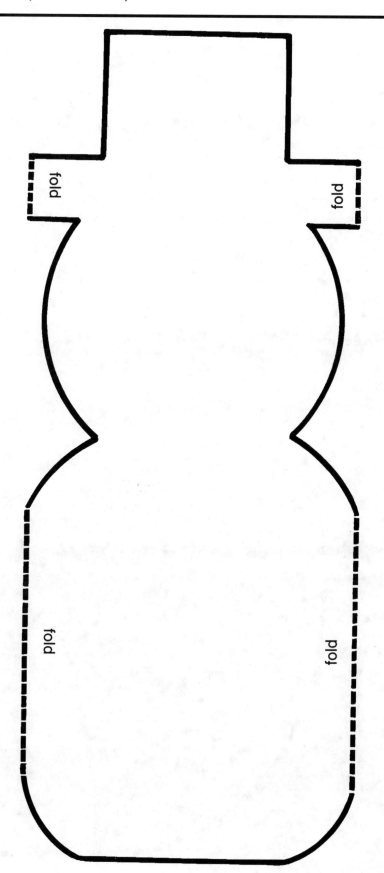

fold

fold

fold

fold

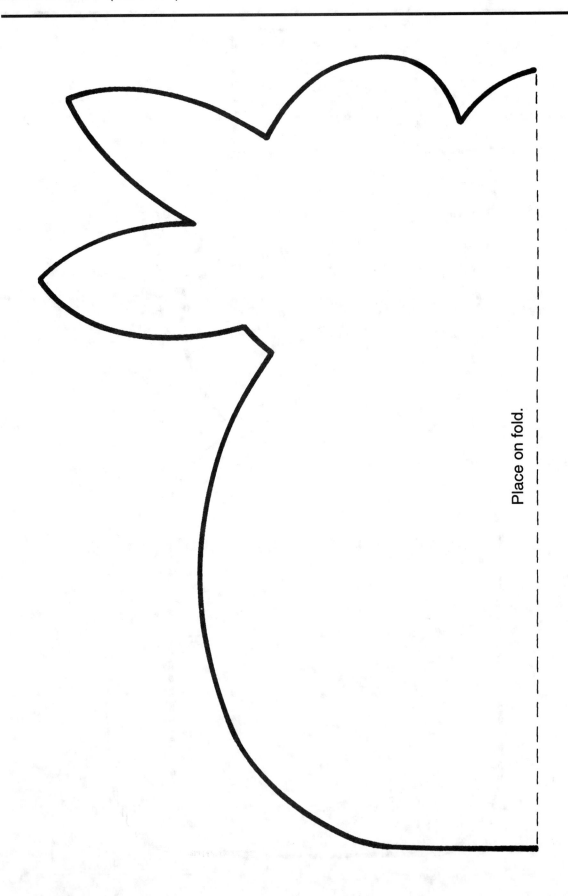

Place on fold.

Butterfly (Slit Book)

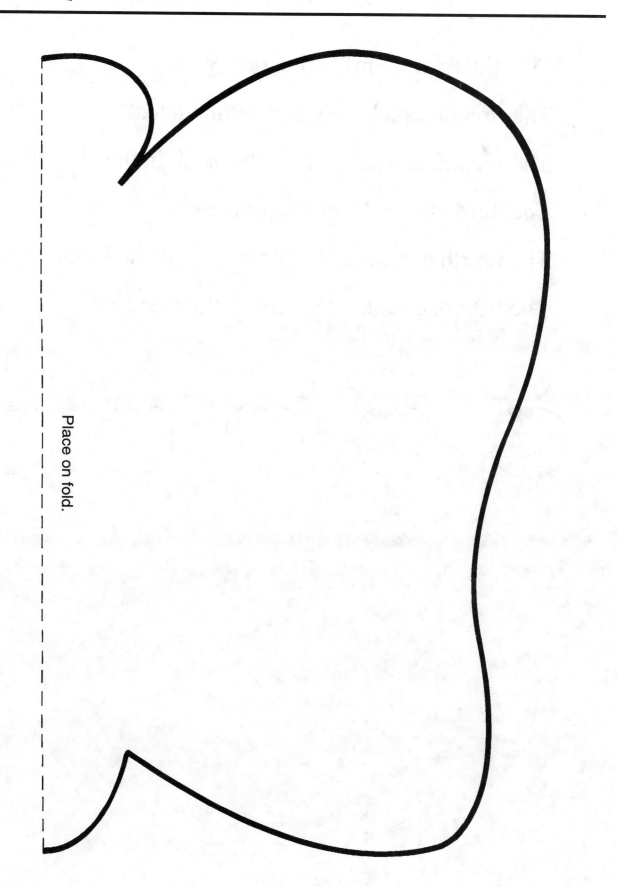

Place on fold.

Five Little Pumpkins

Five little pumpkins sitting on a gate.

The first one said, "My, it's getting late."

The second one said, "There's magic in the air."

The third one said, "We don't care."

The fourth one said, "Let's run and run and run."

The fifth one said, "It's only Halloween fun!"

Teachin' Cheap